D0250807

A GRAMMAR OF THE FILM

A GRAMMAR OF THE FILM

AN ANALYSIS OF FILM TECHNIQUE

By

Raymond Spottiswoode

UNIVERSITY OF CALIFORNIA PRESS
Berkeley and Los Angeles
1969

UNIVERSITY OF CALIFORNIA PRESS
BERKELEY AND LOS ANGELES
CALIFORNIA

SBN   520-01200-3

ORIGINALLY PUBLISHED IN GREAT BRITAIN BY
FABER AND FABER, LIMITED

PRINTED BY OFFSET IN THE UNITED STATES OF AMERICA

A
GILBERTE

Preface

THE READER will not need more than a glance at this
book to discover that it arose out of the ashes of
long-forgotten controversies, and was written at a ten-
der age when the splitting of hairs seemed to its author
more important than making new discoveries. We may
imagine him, as he sat in his paneled Oxford study,
the work for his degree pushed to one side, floor and
table laden with early writings on the film—the work
of such practical masters as Pudovkin, Eisenstein and
Grierson, and the scourings of critics and others whose
names have not survived the years. What had they to
say, these early analysts? Had they established the
theory of the film as a veritable art? Had they sufficiently distinguished it from the art forms out of which
it grew? Above all, had they fully appreciated the
grounds of this distinction?

The young author did not think so. With all the
heady enthusiasm of his twenty years, and unembar-
rassed by any actual contact with film, he felt that he
had the answer. And in a Chart at the end of his book,
which even his closest friends found more than a little
perplexing, he proceeded to set out the twin aspects
of film, Analytic and Synthetic, and show wherein the

1

film maker could diverge or differentiate his representation of nature from the literal rendering to which the medium lent itself with such a fatal facility. The book itself was a clothing of the bare skeleton of this Chart.

Sixteen years have passed. The sound film, which was in 1933 a relatively new experiment, is now a commonplace, and is even, in a world of rapid technical change, seeing its authority threatened by a new expressive medium, television. Yet, as with the other arts, the foundations of film are not really in danger. It has its tools, its skills, its standards, its audience, its masters, its literature. In a word, it has reached maturity. How, then, does this early study of film stand up to the passage of time? Has it any validity when the experimental stage has been passed?

The answer seems to be that film is a medium still so much under commercial domination that it is always in danger of falling into stereotyped forms which are easy to exploit. There is, therefore, a continuing need to go back to fundamentals, and see what new forms can be spun out of the basic substance of film. Never was the need for experiment greater than today, when so little is being done. Thus any study, however imperfect, which tries to lay bare the scaffolding of the film medium, may be able to help the creative worker on his way.

Preface

The author's first chapter sets out his grounds for writing the book, and here we may feel that he more than fully discharges his debt of scholarship to Oxford, and weighs his text down with a mass of distinctions without differences. After this he proceeds to define certain common film terms, and this section does succeed in focusing the reader's mind on those factors which affect the picture image, the sound track, and the film as a whole which is a synthesis of the two.

At this point the book sets out to bring the reader up to date—that is, up to 1933—with a brief history of film. A great many of the films mentioned may be obtained in America from the Museum of Modern Art, and all students of film should consider this an essential part of their training, for films cannot be studied in any other way than by seeing them. Nothing effective in film corresponds to the text of a play or a musical score.

For most of his prognostications in this chapter, the author peered into a very clouded crystal ball. He looked for greater freedom of expression in Russia just at the moment when the first attack on formalism in the arts was launched, and when practically all independence of outlook was to be crushed, never to revive. Though the signs of a renaissance in the French cinema were already apparent with the work of Vigo, Pagnol, and Duvivier, he does not seem to have de-

3

tected them. And the maturity of English feature films was an event still hidden far below the horizon.

On the other hand, close contact with the English documentary film movement enabled the author to recognize fully its importance as a growing point in the search for a realism at once socially valid and economically viable. At the same time, the warnings he gave against the supineness of attitude which often accompanies government control find their echo today in the impotence of U. S. State Department pictures and the current eclipse of British documentary films.

In his fourth chapter, after all these preliminary skirmishes, the author gets to grips with his subject and launches into an elaborate series of abstractions designed to draw attention to film fundamentals. His stress on the distinction between the living personalities of actors on the stage and their shadowy images on the screen seems to need just as much emphasis now as then. Films like *Mourning Becomes Electra* continue to be produced; and television offers a flat and melancholy reminder in many an American home that personality cannot be projected through the ether by a mere representation of the actor's face and gestures.

Having rejected alike the film which is based on the obvious similarities between stage and cinema and the film which is based solely on the cinema's autonomous powers, the author takes up a middle ground which calls for a full exploitation of the medium's resources together with a willingness to accept aid from any and all of the neighboring arts. Though such an eclectic point of view may seem the merest common sense, it is surprising to find that after fifty years of film making it is still unorthodox. Film makers do not for the most part search in the film's arsenal of powers for an apt means of expression. They remain content with its imitative abilities, which lie always and dangerously ready to hand. There are few indeed who, faced with the problem of making a film, are prepared to lay aside conventions and think themselves into the very stuff of their medium, as the poets, painters, and composers of the last sixty years have found it necessary to do.

Film is at once the newest and most conservative of the arts; and this perhaps because it has vigorously taken root in the newest but most conservative of countries, America. Size, so excellent in the abstract, turns out to be the greatest enemy of change. The dinosaur was probably only conscious of his magnificent body until the assaults of the smaller carnivores forced a recognition that he had the most insignificant brain of them all. It seems unhappily true that Hollywood films will prove to be the dinosaur of the arts, immense in physical scale, feeble in wits, ponderously unchangeable when new conditions like the advent of television arise.

Hence it is that the two central chapters of our author's book deserve perhaps a closer attention than their rather dry and pedantic approach would seem to warrant them. They do succeed in digging down to the roots of the subject, at least on the aesthetic side, which is as far as they set out to go. They do succeed in calling attention to those unique powers of the film which are still neglected by the majority of film makers. Many, however, and the present writer among them, will take strong exception to individual statements. Even if there is general agreement that wipes (pp. 121–123) distract from the illusion of a film by drawing attention to the unreality of the film image, it is no reason to rule them out altogether. There are films whose very virtue is their unreality, and which depend on destroying the illusion which camera and continuity make it so easy to establish. The films of Paul Rotha, which abound in wipes, are the most striking examples of this style.

Again, the author is exceedingly wary about the advantages of color (except in animated films) because he fears that it will prove yet another step on the road backward to a mere imitation of life. There is plenty of supporting evidence in the color films of the last sixteen years—but a few, like *Henry V,* have been able to move in the border world between abstraction and reality, and so share in the advantages of both. If the

Preface

stereoscopic film were ever realized, it would seem that it too could enjoy these advantages. There is a world of solid shapes far removed from the luscious figures and glamorous interiors with which Hollywood will fill its stereoscopic movies. And beyond the third dimension looms the fourth. Even within the limits of present space, stereoscopics can become a powerful instrument for transcending reality, not merely imitating it. Some of these possibilities are examined in a later book by the same author, *Film and Its Techniques.*

It is when he arrives at the subject of sound that our author's hair-splitting logic becomes most perplexing. He divides the world of sound into so many categories, subcategories, and sliding scales that the average reader would probably be happier if he were faced with a set of differential equations. However, the theory of the sound film is essentially difficult, and perhaps even fewer people are experimenting with sound now than in 1933, when it was still something of a novelty. It may be useful, therefore, to try to disentangle what the author has to say from the brambles of logic on which it is caught.

The sound film consists of two wholly separate parts: a band of picture images and a sound track. There is no reason whatever why the sound track should reproduce the sounds usually made by the objects represented in the band of images, of which the spoken word is the most obvious. Even here, in fact, a person who has never sung a note of music can be gifted by the film with the most divine voice, men can be made to speak as women, an actor whose lips move in English may be heard in Italian or French. Anything can be made to happen. Expected sounds (doors banging, bands playing, feet shuffling) can be suppressed; unexpected sounds substituted.

All this the author classifies on a scale of realism–nonrealism, going from a literal sound rendering of a scene to a completely nonliteral rendering. He then distinguishes two subscales, or modes in which this variation can be effected. First, in a numerical way, different *sorts* of sounds can be rendered on the realistic or nonrealistic principle. For instance, in a dialogue scene, all natural sounds (moving objects, etc.) might be recorded as in life, but the actual speech of the characters could be suppressed, and replaced by some kind of spoken thoughts. This possibility has been little explored in practice. Secondly, he points out, all recorded sounds may be intensively varied, so that they become either louder or softer than in real life. For instance, a whisper which a guilty and suspicious person picks up in a crowd may be magnified on the sound track a hundred times and repeated over and over again until it becomes a veritable voice of doom.

And finally, introducing his last complication, the author points out that all these modes of variation are susceptible of undergoing yet another, which he calls contrapuntal and noncontrapuntal. By this he means that a sound can either originate from a source which is actually seen in the shot, or from a source outside it but in the real or supposed acoustic field of the microphone. The most obvious example of a noncontrapuntal source of sound is a person who is both seen and heard speaking, as in the average feature film. Even in such films, minor examples of contrapuntal sounds are easy to find: a church bell echoing from the distance, the ticking of a clock on the wall, a telephone bell, a person whose voice comes from outside the frame. But rare indeed, even after twenty-five years of sound film, is an effort to build up a whole ambience of sound, derived from the milieu of the sequence but complementing and not merely echoing what goes on in the scene.

Furthermore, in the general frame of realistic–nonrealistic sound, a choice must be made between representing a scene in a broadly objective way (the fly on the wall), and presenting it through the eyes of one character (e.g., *The Lady in the Lake*). Here, also, the employment of sound is extremely important.

And this brings us to the author's second main scheme of classification, which he calls parallel–

contrastive. This is a psychological scale, ranging from the case in which the sound track simply reinforces the impression conveyed by the shots, or visual images, to that wherein the two produce a violently contrasting effect. At this end of the scale, much experimenting still remains to be done; what was done at the beginning of the sound era has already been forgotten and needs rediscovery.

In the remaining sections of his treatment of sound (pp. 181–193), the author shows how all these uses of sound may be made to interact with one another, and he gives a number of examples from films of the period. But the main value of this section to the student of today is to focus his attention on the many interesting and valuable things which can be done with the film sound track, and which at the moment lie neglected.

Chapter vi of the book turns away from these elements of construction which the film maker and critic should have at their finger tips when considering the aesthetics of a film. The reverse side of the picture is the synthesis whereby the film produces its effect on an audience, and here the author tends to ignore the orthodox means of story continuity and concentrates instead on the peculiar and often-discussed phenomenon of montage. He is at his best in his most general comments, in which he succeeds in showing that it is discontinuity, not continuity, in which resides most of the cinema's special powers. This discontinuity, however, is not a thing *sui generis*, but is merely an extreme heightening of principles of contrast well developed in other arts. Least satisfactory is the analysis of rhythmical montage, which is much influenced by a now unfashionable branch of economics called hedonimetry, or the measurement of satisfactions. While the argument has a general validity, its details probably do not deserve very close attention.

There follows a discussion of other forms of montage, which suffers from an overindulgence of this principle of discontinuity. All obstacles to its use—camera movement, realistic sound, even dialogue itself—tend to be thrust aside in favor of a kind of film which would struggle to express itself entirely by implications and discontinuities. This may well seem a rather doctrinaire approach, and a disregard of the eclectic principles professed in an earlier chapter. After all, the film can render life as it is seen and heard. This should not be regarded as a defect, or even as a last resource, but merely as the basic fabric of film making which must be modified by the various creative tools the medium provides.

The author ends this main section of his book with a classification of theories of art in their bearing on film. Suffice it to say that his description of Marxist aesthetics bears not the slightest resemblance to what is practiced today under that name in the Soviet Union. There, Marxism—like Communism itself—is dead, replaced by a government as reactionary in its attitude to art as to politics and human betterment.

The last chapters survey in rather pedantic detail the different classes in which films may be made to fall by a sufficient exercise of abstraction. This leads up to a definition of documentary films which accords well enough with modern ideas, and of the imagist film, a type which has undergone little development in the turmoil of the latter years. The synthetic (i.e., the animated) film seems to have got stuck on some such rock as the author discovers in its path. For economic reasons, the Disney type of film cartoon has become more and more unimaginative and tasteless. Other types of animated film, many of them developed in Canada, have not yet emerged into the sort of maturity which one could by now expect. They are charming, agreeable, delightful to look at, but rather minor in stature. Whether they have not found a creator, or whether they do not lend themselves to creation on a larger scale, only the future can show.

And so the author takes leave of his subject. Gazing out of his study from between his piles of books onto Oxford's tree-shaded walks and quiet serenity, the world seems a disorderly place, needing the preachments of a professor to set it to rights. Later he may have learned that life does not fit itself into neat compartments, that at all times it is subject to violent whims and changes, and that the arts themselves are the least predictable of human creations. Grammarians, however, are entitled to a little charity. Perhaps without their aid, unrecognized as it is, poets could not write sonnets to their mistresses. And even film makers, struggling to overcome a thousand hampering conditions, may owe them something for pointing out new ways of advance.

R. J. S.

Territet, Switzerland
August, 1949.

Contents

15

Contents

Contents

CHAPTER IV—CATEGORIES OF THE FILM
a. DISTINCTIONS

CHAPTER V—TECHNIQUE OF THE FILM
1. ANALYSIS

17

Contents

Contents

Chapter VI—Technique of the Film
2. Synthesis

Contents

Contents

Contents

Acknowledgments

IN THE ORIGINAL EDITION the author acknowledged his indebtedness to the writings of Mr. Paul Rotha, well-known film maker and historian, and of Miss C. A. Lejeune, then as now film critic of the London *Observer,* and one of the wittiest and most unsparingly honest of writers on the film. Mr. R. F. G. Ormrod and Mr. J. F. Coplestone-Boughey were responsible for many suggestions incorporated in the book, for which Mr. A. R. Norton prepared the index. Above all, the author's gratitude was due to one who wished only to be known under the initials E. C. M., but "whose encouragement and criticism [had] made the task of writing an enjoyment and the quest for new material an adventure."

Chapter I

Introductory

'When *I* use a word', Humpty Dumpty said in rather a scornful tone, 'it means just what I choose it to mean—neither more nor less.'

'The question is', said Alice, 'whether you can make words mean different things.'

'The question is', said Humpty Dumpty, 'which is to be master—that's all.'

LEWIS CARROLL

---

1. *Confusions of film controversy*. 2. *Aims of the present study*. 3. *The purpose of illustrations and examples*. 4. *The balance between assumption and verification*. 5. *The value of distinctions*. 6. *The domains of scientific and philosophical definition*.

---

1. The number of books devoted to the cinema is already so great that the appearance of another must be a matter for excuse. Many sides of the subject have been treated from many different angles: the writing of scenarios, the duties of directors, the history of the film and its relation to other arts, the correct treatment of sound and the correct development of technique. It would be regrettable if an art-form as young as the film were to give rise

to no controversy and discover no new problems. But it is equally regrettable that out of this welter of dispute nothing but a few vague names should have emerged. Eisenstein distinguishes five types of montage,[1] while Mr. Dalton, writing in a prominent English film magazine,[2] denies altogether that montage exists. The true relation of cinema to stage is so little understood that the screen play is hopefully pursued in one direction and the abstract film in the other. There are writers who assign the choice of camera-angle to the mood of the director and the subject of his scene;[3] while others give it a mathematical fixity.[4] While some people affect to find in the cinema the greatest art-form of to-day,[5] and its productions among the greatest modern works of art, others, at least as intelligent, denounce it as the resort of none but 'celluloid nit-wits',[6] or at best are surprised to hear that films are not all made in factories, and that men have even turned instinctively to the cinema as the medium best adapted to their creative powers.

[1] *Close-Up*, April 1930.

[2] *Cinema Quarterly*, vol. 1, no. 2. Discussed pp. 193-196 below.

[3] Arnheim, *Film*, pp. 59-60. Quoted p. 132 below.

[4] Hunter, *Scrutiny of Cinema*, p. 21. Discussed pp. 135-137 below.

[5] Pudovkin, *Film Technique*, pp. 173-174. Discussed pp. 311-312 below.

[6] *E.g.* Mr. St. John Ervine. See pp. 309-311 below.

The cinema has been undermined on opposite sides. The intelligentsia have wrapped it in a learned obscurity, hoping to gain a monopoly of wisdom by a manufacture of knowledge. Commercial magnates, as satisfied by an art imposed on the people as by one which has sprung naturally from them, have made their appeal to a lowest common denominator of mankind, fearing that some might be so stupid as to miss what none would rightly, but for them, have cared to learn. It is small wonder, then, that the art of the cinema, having inclined in many directions, now shows signs of falling altogether. To this collapse its exponents and friends have contributed. When a new school of painting defines its art in extravagant terms, there is no danger of discredit to the whole art; but the cinema is not yet established, and the outside critic may be forgiven a smile at the quarrels carried on with strange and various vocabularies over an art which may not exist and has certainly not produced any works of lasting importance.

The recent translation into English of Herr Arnheim's book *Film Als Kunst*[1] has done something to mitigate this confusion. But *Film* was written at a time when, as the author confesses, sixty per cent of the speech in German cinemas was unintelligible,

[1] Published in England under the title *Film*. References throughout are to the English edition.

and it is therefore not surprising that many of its predictions in relation to the sound film have not been fulfilled. Moreover, Herr Arnheim vacillates between championing either the sound or silent cinema, and thus compromises his account of the relation between them. But to-day the silent film has not only disappeared as a practical consideration; sound films have vindicated themselves as having all, and more than all, the potentialities of their predecessors. Nevertheless, Parts II and III of *Film* contain an analysis of the relation between what is seen and what is shot, which is not likely to be soon surpassed. This work must be the basis of all future accounts of cinema technique, as it is of that study of the individual shot which is one of the main subjects of this book.

Before proceeding, it will be well to answer an objection which, though levelled at *Film*, is still more applicable to the present work. Miss Lejeune[1] criticizes Herr Arnheim for accepting the fallacy 'post hoc, ergo propter hoc'; by merely seeing films instead of making them, he is led to read into them the fruit of his theories, when in fact they are only the result of happy accident or commercial pressure. But to this it may be answered that the artist often works better than he knows. His task is to bring to a focus and materialize some aspect of life which has

[1] *The Observer.*

28

interested him, whether he follows his natural inclinations or submits to the dictation of external circumstances. In neither case does he necessarily dissect and separate his means; indeed, criticism and creation are often most fully developed when most fully divorced. The critic makes clear the way of appreciation by pointing out the links and processes which the artist overleaped.

2. It is the aim of this book to make as precise as possible the language and grammar which the film, as a prospective art-form, has to acquire; next, to outline its history, redressing the balance of criticism which has inevitably but wrongly laid sole stress on the machine-made film, and indicating the economic and political factors which have determined its course in the past and are likely to influence it in the future; then to discuss various lines of development in the cinema, considering some immediately, deferring others for discussion in later chapters, and selecting one—the most profitable—for detailed treatment and analysis. This is treated first as a material structure and then as an artistic unity, both in its visual aspect and in its organic relationship to sound. Finally a return is made to the types of film, notably the documentary, which can be given fuller treatment in the light of preceding chapters; and an attempt to strike a mean between extremes of praise and blame of the cinema brings the book to an end.

None of the problems raised receives any final solution, for the maturity of an art enlarges horizons as soon as it widens understanding. It will be enough to have established the cinema, its language and grammar, on a basis of common agreement, so that discussion may build on substance instead of battling with empty words. It is therefore of less importance that many arguments are pursued only a few stages; the reader is either referred to a fuller discussion elsewhere, or encouraged to proceed securely himself. A balanced and synoptic view of the cinema not only allows existing treatments of it to be estimated and related, but prevents an advance along one line at the expense of regression in another. Where the argument deals in scientific terms, it can be added to in future (*e.g.* if the 'solid' film comes into common use) without much modification in the main theory; but where its treatment is philosophical, as it at present stands at the head of and sums up existing systems, so it will in its turn be embodied by successors in new and basically different schemes of thought. The scientist adds wings and extensions to his building; the philosopher refashions it in each generation after the manner of a mediaeval cathedral.[1] The philosophic and scientific approaches are at one, however, in being subject to

[1] R. G. Collingwood, *An Essay on Philosophical Method*, chapter ix.

drastic alteration when presented with conflicting facts. Aesthetic theory is a consistent structure built up on and harmonizing particular aesthetic judgments; it is not an *a priori* scheme from which these judgments can be logically deduced. The contrary instance cannot be treated in Hume's cavalier manner: 'It is so particular and singular, that 'tis scarce worth our observing, and does not merit that, for it alone, we should alter our general maxim.'[1]

3. Illustrations of points in the text are given from well-known films; if every reader were to be thus convinced of each point by direct appeal, the text would be encumbered with names; but if all such names were omitted, long verbal descriptions would have to replace them. It is hoped that a satisfactory compromise has been made and that, wherever possible, the reader will consult his own experience of films, so that a brief allusion will be sufficient to bring a vivid picture to his mind, and either convince him of the validity of a theoretical argument, or provide him with material for contending it. No attempt, however, has been made to provide subtle or detailed examples of the general principles enumerated. Mr. John Grierson, in describing Pudovkin's examples of asynchronism as 'curiously shallow',[2]

[1] *Treatise on Human Nature*, i. 1, sec. 1.
[2] *Cinema Quarterly*, winter 1933-34, pp. 106-107.

apparently misunderstands their purpose. They are aids to the reader who, finding it difficult to relate written theory to practised fact, loses the thread of the discourse in clouds of woolly abstraction. They are not intended to exhaust the instances of the laws they illustrate. That is the work of the creative artist; and the dangers of its application to theory are well displayed in *Film*, where Herr Arnheim, in the praiseworthy endeavour to temper the severity of theoretical reasoning, is forced into long descriptions of actual shots and sequences, which seldom rise above the level of chronicles of fact. In the following pages, however, the examples are avowedly crude; and in the expectation that the reader will envisage more instances of a principle than are described, the thesis has been compressed and shortened; but, to exhibit it at a glance in its entirety, a chart has been prepared. This chart is not intended to assist any proof, still less to draw attention to any uniformity of relationship. Thus, by contrast, the links which connect the parts of a genealogical tree have unique significances; so that, once their number and sense are known, the relationship between their terminal points may be accurately apprehended; but in the chart, links represent a great multiplicity of types of relationship, which cannot be determined by inspection. With this warning, the chart will be found to present the structure of the argument very clearly;

but, as it gives no precise indication of the order in which subjects are treated below, an analytical table of contents is appended.

There is a danger that the 'stills' which accompany books on the cinema may be rated at more than their proper value; those which are beautiful tend to distract a reader who has not yet grasped the subject from the truth that the value of a film is not necessarily in proportion to the value of the shots which compose it (e.g. *La Passion de Jeanne d'Arc* and *The Blue Light*).

4. The study of the cinema must ultimately take a place within the province of the science of aesthetics.[1] Then and only then, as has been the case with other sciences, will it be profitable to divide it into a pure and an applied branch. The danger of too early a dichotomy is shown by the example of economics, which has advanced incomparably nearer the status of an exact science than has the study of the film. The true scope of economics is still hotly disputed

---

[1]Here and elsewhere this word is not given its usual significance, but is intended as a translation of the German *Kunstforschung*, which has no counterpart in our language. The meaning is the body of studies of art, of which history is only a section. Mr. Roger Fry's term *art-history* is preferable to *aesthetics* in that it does not distort an accepted usage; but it is inferior for our purpose here, where little emphasis is laid on the historical aspects of the subject (see Mr. Fry's *Art-History as an Academic Study*, pp. 5-12).

between the Institutionalists, who are chiefly concerned with the collection and collation of statistical data, and the pure theorists, who are unwilling to forsake the strict certainty of science for the caprices of human nature.[1] Thus, solely to emphasize either, for example, the dimensional conflict which lends an air of unreality to the drawn film,[2] or the cost and number of the productions of Hollywood, would be to invite the charge of academic theorizing on the one hand, and of crude empiricism on the other. The aim of the writer, however imperfectly fulfilled, should be to concede enough certainty to make his conclusions applicable to the real world, and at the same time to press forward his analysis far enough to transcend the temporary value of a mere collection of facts. This balance can be struck by a judicious combination of inductive and deductive methods; though in aesthetics induction is of lesser value. In economics, on the other hand, the ceaseless refinements of analysis are of great value because, though they are now limited by unreal assumptions, they will ultimately be applicable to the real world. The condition of this practical usefulness is the size of the group to which general laws are applied; the

[1] See Prof. Robbins, *The Nature and Significance of Economic Science*, and the reply by Mr. Fraser, *Economic Journal*, Dec. 1932, p. 555.
[2] See pp. 304-305 below.

larger it is the more will individual peculiarities be cancelled, and the sharp edge of economic distinctions remain unblunted. Aesthetics, however, if we except the study of advertisement, deals almost exclusively with personal reactions, which are subject to endless variation, particularly in the domain of art. The resources of introspection provide a fairly clear insight into the reactions of a single being, and to these a logical method of analysis may be applied. But to generalize from such slender premises is to simplify dangerously. Close reasoning will be upset by prejudice and by differences of outlook and training. Only a broad outline can stand firm.

5. Distinctions, therefore, cannot be used to establish laws. But they are invaluable in complicated situations where the importance to be assigned to a single element is difficult to determine. The method of *ceteris paribus* (one of the great engines of economic thought) distinguishes the necessary components of the situation and immobilizes all but one of them, whose influence it then examines. Thus one by one each factor is freed until the whole problem becomes soluble; and prejudice, which usually stifles appreciation by violently inhibiting it, is checked at the very start. The value of the work of art which is being dissected cannot indeed be measured by these simple means; but, even had we no standards, we could better discriminate the weights

35

of 999 hairs and of 1000 if we protected our scales from the external influence of air-currents, balanced the beam with a micrometer screw, and fashioned the knife-edges of a material which was not appropriate to the other parts. The appreciation of art increases with the power of discrimination. This is most clearly seen in the case of wines; the connoisseur who can distinguish between two neighbouring vintages is also as a rule keener in his enjoyment of either than the man to whose palate they appear the same. Only less clear is the principle in the art of choosing words. The unpractised writer will discover a great number of groups of words whose components appear to him synonymous, so that his choice between them is conditioned only by accidental circumstance. As his experience and sensibility increase, however, he appreciates a widening penumbra of association surrounding each word and contracting the free space in which his selection is indeterminate; at the same time, his powers of communication are enriched; the overtones which poets and philosophers have contributed to language convey more than he directly expresses; and finally, when almost every word has taken on a separate significance, he will not need a very wide vocabulary to express a great range of thought and feeling.[1]

[1]In the same way, economists have come to realize that the older conception of a commodity concealed a multitude of

It is likely that these results hold good for every form of artistic appreciation; and even though finer discrimination be a concomitant rather than a cause of heightened enjoyment, it would seem better to train the understanding by rational exercise than to wait passively for an increase of sensibility. In the domain of religious experience, there are some who immediately and without effort can come before the presence of God; but the majority must by reasoning and power of will surmount the obstacles to faith, and subject their spirits to the discipline of fasting and prayer. So also with art. The most intense enjoyment is not theirs who cast off learning for a child's simplicity; but theirs who, in the bearing of such simplicity, come armed with every power of the mind.

6. Criticism and the study of technique may thus be justified even to those who grant them little value in themselves, and deny that they can be of any assistance in the process of artistic understanding. Such a view commends itself to the empirical English mind; and it is fostered by too strict attention to terminology. Some writers have indeed believed that

heterogeneous elements, small in themselves, but important in the aggregate. A greater power of subdivision has enabled them to reduce the field of error; a practice which is shown below to apply to the cinema, particularly in relation to margins and volumes of indifference, in the treatment of camera-angles (see pp. 133-135 below).

studious vagueness is the condition of aesthetic appreciation; but even by more moderate standards, it will seem dangerous to straitlace an art by very precise definition and rigorous insistence on a norm.

On the other hand, the greater number of critical controversies over the film are mere matters of definition and temperament. The term 'documentary', though it has not the venerable history of confusion and dispute which lies behind 'romantic', is now the subject of hot dissension. Those who champion documentary films tacitly define their scope as coincident with almost all that is good in the contemporary cinema. Their opponents, who would never challenge this contention if they properly understood its basis, confine the term to what they, and the other party as well, regard as affected and pretentious. There can be no agreement until the issues are impartially set out, and the word 'documentary' given a clear and colourless connotation.[1] It is one of the aims of this book to do such a service for the cinema in general. In Chapter II a series of definitions is given, the members of which fall generally into two classes, though closer inspection will show them to extend between two logical limits. First are the terms which express a mathematical fact about which there can be no dispute, except between witless persons. Thus 'slow-motion' means 'the passage

[1]See pp. 288-296 below.

of the film through the camera more quickly than through the projector'. Of the second class is the 'temporal close-up', which denotes 'a close-up in time instead of space, contrived so that parts only of a movement are arrested by slow-motion in order to heighten their significance'. The first class of definition, though necessary, has only a very limited use, and does not form a vital part of the criticism of art itself. Its value lies in making comprehensible the definitions of the second class. Not until the mechanical principle of slow-motion is understood can the nature of the temporal close-up be conceived at all; even then, however, it cannot be declared artistically justified on the basis of a short definition such as that given above. It is therefore necessary to make constant reference to the temporal close-up, in order that the first meagre description may be overlaid and filled out by subsequent associations. Only then will it be possible to argue that such a close-up corresponds to the state of mind of the artist at the moment when his inspiration seizes on some object as fit for his artistic powers to embody; and that it is therefore a valuable means of communication.[1] The condensation of definitions into two classes is, of course, only an expository device; in fact, there are imperceptible stages of definition, ascending from the more to the less scientific, by which we arrive at

[1]The argument is set out pp. 164-166 below.

this position. Once having arrived, we can only appeal to the experience of the individual to confirm or deny a particular conclusion. Agreement will establish the point over a certain field; disagreement will have revealed a fundamental divergence of temperament between writer and reader. Here we reach the second cause of dispute mentioned above; and no further progress can be made. But it is essential that this stage should be reached, in order to make perfectly clear why reconciliation is impossible.

Between strictness and indeterminacy, rigidity of logical structure and formlessness, a middle way must be found. The one set of extremes determines the exact rightness or wrongness of conflicting views, but suffers the disabilities of dogmatism and prevents the expansion of unforeseen knowledge and experience; the other welcomes all that is new, but loses its way and wastes the energy of its exponents in futile and unnecessary quarrels.

Criticism and the study of technique are thus justified against those who deny their contribution to enjoyment, and those who point scornfully to the strife they have set up. But they are not justified against those who deny their place in artistic creation. Here argument fails; creative processes are so rarely described by the artist at all, still more rarely in relation to the furnishings of his own mind, that there is place only for vain speculation. Many artists no doubt have their private theories to help them; but the publication of these, especially by men who had not made a profession of logical thought, would be valueless. Criticism halts at the gate of creation; but art, being born of the need to communicate, has a double nature; it can be half fulfilled in coming into being, without the aid of generally accepted theory; but it is half lost unless it is understood and enjoyed; and the furtherance of understanding and enjoyment is the business of criticism.

Chapter II

Definitions

'And all a rhetorician's rules
Teach nothing but to name his tools.'
SAMUEL BUTLER: *Hudibras*

---

*The total film (C) comprises a visual film (A) and
a sound factor (B). A. The visual film—(a) the film
material: the mechanical principle, speeds, cutting,
dissolves, fades; (b) The camera: positions and movements; (c) illusion: filmic space and time, trick
processes; (d) description: titles of various types.
B. The sound factor—(a) speech: realistic and unrealistic uses; (b) sound: realistic and unrealistic
uses; (c) music: realistic and unrealistic uses. C. The
total film—(a) construction: different types of
montage; (b) categories: different types of film; (c)
effect: different types of effect produced by the film
and its component parts.*

In this chapter it is proposed to state technicalities
rather than discuss techniques. Certain basic
terms, denoting the mechanical processes of the
cinema, do not relate to its sphere and methods as an
art, but to the tools with which the images of physical objects are selected, composed and if necessary

distorted, and finally recorded on celluloid. Others again relate to the application of sound and speech to the film, or connote the psychological effects of the film as a whole. Technique is based on the choice of these tools; it cannot be theoretically considered without a clear understanding of them, nor be practically employed unless their material nature is familiar.

The first type of knowledge is mainly needed here. It is more important to relate the terms defined in a general framework than to pile up definitions which would be superfluous in a first consideration of technique. While meagre definitions would result in ambiguity, full explanations would prejudge later issues. Most of the following terms, therefore, are those in current use in the sphere of film production. The few terms which have been coined are given in their appearance a wide meaning, and merely suggest the special significance which results from subsequent discussion.

THE TOTAL FILM. The complete film as it is known to-day. It is composed of

THE VISUAL FILM, or part which is projected on a screen and seen by the spectator, and

A SOUND FACTOR, or part which is reproduced by loud-speakers and heard by the spectator.

Definitions

A. THE VISUAL FILM

a. The film material.

The strip of film which is exposed in the film camera. After development and printing, this strip, or a copy of it, is passed through the projector.

1. *The mechanical principle of the visual film.* Photographs (called *frames*) are taken in series at regular intervals of time. When projected on a screen at a rate of sixteen or more frames per second, they produce, by persistence of vision, an illusion of continuity. If the time-intervals of taking and projecting are the same, the rates of movement of an object as it is filmed and projected will also be the same.

2. *Fast motion.* The film is passed through the camera more slowly than through the projector. Thus an object moves faster when projected than when filmed.

3. *Slow motion.* The film is passed through the camera more quickly than through the projector. Thus an object moves slower when projected than when filmed.

4. *The shot.* A portion of film portraying physical objects without visible spatial or temporal discontinuity.

5. *The cut.* The instantaneous transference from any shot to its successor.

6. *Rate of cutting.* Measured by the number of shots which occupy a given length of film and hence a given time of projection (rate of projection being in practice constant). Rate of cutting is said to be slow when these shots are long, fast when they are short, and positively or negatively accelerated for shots which become shorter or longer respectively as the fixed length of film proceeds.

The transference from shot to shot may be effected by other means than the cut:

7. *The dissolve.* The second shot appears on the screen seemingly under the first and becomes increasingly distinct. The first shot then becomes decreasingly distinct and disappears. Dissolves are called quick and slow according to the time occupied by this process.

8. *The wipe.* The first shot is peeled off, revealing the second as if it had lain previously beneath it. Wipes may be distinguished into left, right, upward and downward according to their starting-point or direction; many other types exist and may be readily envisaged.

9. *Fade out and in.* The light-intensity of the first shot falls to zero, and that of the second rises thereupon to its normal value. The first part of the process is called a Fade, and a Slow Fade if it occupies more than the usual time.

b. The camera.

The composition of a shot is governed by:

1. *Camera position.* The position of the camera referred to axes through the centre of attention of the subject.

2. *Camera angle.* The angle between the optical axis of the camera and the implied horizontal of the subject. If great accuracy of statement is not required, this term embraces the preceding.

If the composition of a shot is fixed, it may be described as follows:

3. *Long shot.* The subject of the shot is apparently remote from the camera. Middle Shot and Close Shot, with other similar terms, have corresponding meanings.

4. *Spatial close-up.* A single object, often a head, is enlarged above its normal size by optical or mechanical means in the camera. The word 'spatial' is often omitted when there is no danger of ambiguity.

5. *Temporal close-up.* A significant part of a movement is arrested in relation to the remainder of the movement by the application of slow-motion.

The composition of a shot may be varied by the following means:

6. *Tracking.* The camera is moved bodily up to its subject.

46

7. *Panning*. The camera pivots round on a vertical axis, taking a panoramic view of its subject.

8. *Tilting*. The camera pivots on the horizontal axis normal to its optical axis.

c. Illusion.

Means by which the film is made independent of a realistic recording of events and objects. (1) and (2) are most important and most characteristic of the film, for they achieve illusory ends by means not purely illusive.

1. *Filmic space.* A selection of shots taken at points geographically remote from one another may, if they do not contain any means of geographical identification, be combined in a new spatial framework; the process by which this is done is called *relational cutting*.

2. *Filmic time.* By the use of fast and slow motion and cutting, time will appear to pass at widely different rates in relation to the subject of the film, under the control of the director.

3. *The Dunning and Schüfftan processes.* Optical means whereby objects actually remote from one another may be fixed in visible relationship within the bounds of a single shot.

4. *Back projection.* The same end may be achieved by projecting from behind on to a screen scenes pre-

viously shot with a film camera; they now form part
of a second camera's subject (*e.g.* the views passing
railway-carriage windows).

d. Description.

Literary means for explaining the purpose, action
or production of a film.

1. *Credit titles.* Wording incorporated into shots at
the beginning of a film to supply its title and the
names of its production staff and cast.

2. *Continuity titles.* Wording interposed in the
film to record speech or to explain action.

3. *Split titles.* Continuity titles in which sentences
are broken up by the interposition of shots.

4. *Moving titles.* Continuity titles which expand,
contract or in any other ways move over the face of
the screen.

5. *Strip titles.* Wording superimposed on a shot
along the lower edge of the screen, and usually intended to translate dialogue in a foreign language.

B. The Sound Factor

a. Speech.

The synchronization of speech with the visual
film.

1. *Realistic use.* The voices and visual impressions
of characters are simultaneously recorded.

2. *Selective use.* The voices and visual impressions of characters may be freely transposed or suppressed.

3. *Commentative use.* A single voice explains and comments on the action of the visual film.

4. *Tonal use.* Speech, often in a language unknown to the audience, is used for its value as sound divorced from sense.

b. Natural sound.

The synchronization with the visual film of any sound, except speech and the sounds of musical instruments. Music may, however, be introduced under (1) below, where realism demands it.

1. *Realistic use.* The sounds produced by the subject of each shot are synchronized with its visual impression.

2. *Selective use.* Sounds may be used independently of any visual record of their sources, and be transposedly combined with the visual film.

c. Music.

A musical score, either already existing or specially composed, is synchronized with the visual film. The following divisions may be used for the most part simultaneously or successively in a single film, or they may occur alone.

1. *Imitative use.* The score imitates natural sounds or the tonal use of speech.

2. *Commentative use.* The score takes the part of a spectator commenting on the visual film, usually ironically.

3. *Evocative use.* The synchronized score is given its fullest positive value. Silence as well as sound is deliberate. *Leitmotifs* act as emotives and assist the visual film towards insight into the characters they are attached to.

4. *Contrastive use.* Does not stand alone but is combined with (2) and (3). The score contrasts with, and so may heighten the effect of, the visual film.

5. *Dynamic use.* A dynamic correspondence of sight and sound brings out the rhythm of cutting rates.

C. THE TOTAL FILM
a. Construction.
The meaning of (1) to (10) will be made more intelligible in the course of Chapters V and VI.

1. *Scenario.* The written teleological and descriptive plan of a film.

2. *Series.* A succession of shots forming a single completed rhythm of sight and sound.

3. *Sequence.* A succession of shots forming, in the complete film, a subordinate unity of conception and purpose.

4. *Montage*. In its effectual aspect,[1] the production of a concept or sensation through the mutual impact of other concepts or sensations; and in its structural aspect, the juxtaposition of shots, series and sequences in such a way as to produce this impact.

5. *Primary montage*. Montage of the concepts derived from observing the contents of successive shots.

6. *Simultaneous montage*. Montage of the concepts derived from shots and the sounds contemporaneous with them on the film.

7. *Rhythmical montage*. Montage of a rhythmical series of cuts, abstracting the effects of the shots which divide them.

8. *Secondary montage*. The means whereby the secondary elements of the film, cutting-tone,[1] content-tone[1] and the effects of sound, are enabled to generate the effects produced by the series.

9. *Implicational montage*. Montage of the concepts derived from observing the sequences regarded as wholes, by way of a realization of the *implications* of these sequences.

10. *Ideological montage*. Montage resulting from the clash of a concept derived from some element in the film with a concept forming part of the observer's ideology.

[1]For definition, see p. 53.

b. Categories.

Under the general heading *Film* are included the categories chiefly discussed in Chapters V and VI. They range from acted studio films to studies of natural types in native surroundings. The following are categories which may be usefully distinguished from these.

1. *The news-reel.* Has no other aim than the quick recording of current events.

2. *The lecture-film.* This is purely instructive. It does not attempt to dramatize, and its montage is either arbitrary or adapted only to the exigencies of the spoken commentary.

3. *The photo-play.* The exact transference of a stage-play to the screen. Camera angle and position are fixed throughout, and there is consequently no cutting or montage of types (5), (7) and (8).

4. *The screen-play.* The camera is brought into active use, but montage is subordinate to continuity of speech, and effect relies on the personality of the actors.

5. *The synthetic film.* A film whose material resembles only in the smallest degree the grouping of natural objects in the world. Its chief quality is therefore *arrangement*, and it may be subdivided according to the purpose to which this arrangement is put. Thus,

6. *The abstract film* employs a purposive arrangement, but one still bearing little resemblance to the natural world, and

7. *The cartoon* approaches some way towards naturalism, and uses flat images, cut or drawn to human and animal shape, for the purpose of fantasy and farce. The sound factor as a rule is dynamic, and the visual film sometimes coloured.

c. Effect.

The following terms refer to the effect produced by the film on the spectator.

1. *Affective tone.* The total psychological change produced either by the whole shot, series, sequence or complete film under discussion, or by some specified factor in them.

2. *Affective factor.* Some analysable constituent of the total film which is capable of producing affective tone.

3. *Cutting-tone.* The affective tone which, as is argued below, is produced solely by rate of cutting, through the agency of rhythmical montage.

4. *Content-tone.* The affective tone produced by components of the subject of shots: *e.g.* line, composition, meaning in the context of the film, etc. These are affective factors in producing content-tone, while content and cutting are affective factors in producing affective tone.

Chapter III

An Outline of Film History

'Knowledges are as pyramids, whereof history is the basis.'
BACON: *Advancement of Learning*

1. *Absence of film classics related to historical and economic causes.* 2. *The earliest developments.* 3. *Germany* (1919-1925). 4. *Russia* (1920-1930). 5. *Germany* (*Pabst*). 6. *America* (*Chaplin*). 7. *France* (*Clair*). 8. *England* (*Asquith*). 9. *Hollywood and the advent of sound.* 10. *America.* 11. *Germany* (1929-1934—*Pabst*). 12. *France* (1929-1934). 13. *Russia* (1930-1934). 14. *The advance-guard* (1920-1933). 15. *The G.P.O. Film Unit.* 16. *The interaction of personal, economic and political factors in film production.*

1. Each generation finds a difficulty in assessing the value of contemporary works of art. The majority of men are so bounded by the present that they cannot achieve the detached view necessary to appreciate tendencies which at first seem shocking or strange. New movements of importance, tending to give a fresh impetus and direction to thought, are as commonly resented by those whose opinions are rooted in the past as they are

54

indiscriminately praised by all who have cast off traditions as mere impediments to progress.

Nevertheless, in the greater number of arts there are works whose origin is so remote that they have freed themselves from the passing arguments and irritations which at first beset them. These are the materials which, in each generation, are constituted into a body of good taste by those who are able to discover in them new enjoyments and application to new needs. But such men of good taste have an advantage over the generations which saw the birth of genius, in that in the passage of time the competitors and imitators of the great have gradually fallen into obscurity; as the highest trees in a thick forest are hardly distinguished from others until the bushes and lower trees are cleared away.

But the cinema is in its first generation. Directors like Chaplin and Griffith, who first realized the possibilities of surprise and close approach, are now making fresh and less obvious discoveries. The forces of invention and the stimulus of commercial development have urged on the technical advance of the film, when common sense would have called a halt to explore existing possibilities and consolidate the position of the art. The sound film succeeded the silent long before the exhaustion of the simpler branch demanded its supersession. To-day there are rumours of the launching of the stereoscopic film, which would sweep away many of the discoveries centred round the process of cutting, itself only lately reinstated as an independent entity after the landslide of the silent film.

This rapid and feverish change is inevitable in an art which waits on the favour of the people and slavishly follows every craze for novelty. Pens and paper are cheap; and an advance in the art of writing, though it might be held up for a time by the conservatism of publishers, could not long be withstood. But the production of films is costly, for it involves not only the hiring of many actors and technicians, but the payment of overhead charges on a mass of necessary equipment. The public has been induced to regard bright lighting and well-oiled efficiency as the criteria of excellence, for what is merely expensive is the cheapest way to success. It may well be that these qualities will have to be forgone if the present standard of films is to be raised. There are many directors whose work is not tawdry enough to please millions, but who might pay their way if they devoted little enough of their resources to the advantages of good lighting and well-known casts, and exhibited their work at small and specialized cinemas where their merits might be properly appreciated.

At the present time there is no film which has had the full approval and enjoyment of sufficient persons of trained sensibility and intelligence to deserve the name of classic. Nevertheless, the output of the meretricious and worthless is so great that any film which shows a sufficient degree of sincerity and competence to be regarded as no more than mediocre in another art is immediately hailed a 'classic of the screen'. The history of the cinema is studded with films which will be remembered because they mark the occasion of technical change, more often forced than spontaneous; there are few which reveal the working of genius, and none probably which will be regarded as true classics by future generations. Thus it is too early to assess the place of the cinema among the arts: all that can be done is to indicate where such talent has arisen that, given a maturer medium to work in, it would have achieved a lasting fame.

2. The cinema was invented some time before its commercial possibilities were realized. There was thus an interval during which a number of special effects were devised and applied, as may be seen in films of the period 1895-1900.[1] But in 1905 the first connected and dramatic narrative was told,[2] and thenceforth the cinema became subservient to the stage, a means of reproduction, even if hampered by defects. There was no attempt at expression through the camera, which was fixed at eye level in the mid-

[1] E.g. *The Child's Dream* and *The Toymaker's Dream*.
[2] *The Great Train Robbery*.

dle of the set, and afterwards held perfectly still. The characters recited their parts, but exaggerated their gestures in order to produce some effect upon this inconveniently deaf machine. To watch Sarah Bernhardt in *Queen Elizabeth* or *La Dame aux Camellias* (the only living form in which she can still be seen) is painful and pathetic. But though the considerable distance between actor and camera, combined with the poor lighting and definition then obtainable, made the greatest appear grotesque, this unhealthy tradition persisted until the early years of the war.

It was then that a second line of development impinged upon and almost transformed the first. Slapstick comedy had found in the cinema a battery of new devices: fast motion made the pompous appear comic; in disappearances objects really vanished, instead of being removed by springs and concealed drawers; reversed film caused whatever had been smashed to fly together again. These emancipations may not have been worthily used; but it is to slapstick that we owe Chaplin and much of the free use of the camera; while from the new amalgam of style and subject already referred to arose the great epics of D. W. Griffith, which gave the cinema its first sense of commanding breadth. They, together with the Italian *Quo Vadis* (1912), set the evil precedent of 'super-productions'; but they attempted to convey ideas which no small resources could have embodied, and which no magnate of to-day would consider.[1]

The advent of war disabled the small beginnings of a European film industry; and the Americans seized the opportunity of increasing their own output so that it could cope with the demands of foreign countries as well as of their own. The result was disastrous. The standard of American films fell; and for the wide conceptions of Griffith were substituted a metallic and superficial glitter. The European public, ignorant of both the possibilities and the achievements of the cinema, and driven by the horrors of the war into abandonment of all standards of morality and taste, accepted with delight the cheap sensations which America offered. Disillusionment was combated by a drug which was not less insidious for being more apparently innocent than excesses of dancing and champagne; and so dominant was the control of business and propaganda over minds sapped of their resistance and powers of revolt that the public is still dulled after fifteen years by the imbecilities it once welcomed, and the cinema still imprisoned when it could take its place in a resurrection of artistic life.

3. But while this process was going on in England, America, Italy and France, a revival was on foot in

[1]But cf. the film of H. G. Wells's *The Shape of Things to Come* for signs of a more enterprising tendency.

Germany. *The Cabinet of Dr. Caligari* (1919) revealed for the first time the possibilities of distortion. Concentrating on the portrayal of the world through a madman's eyes, it used every device of pattern, light and shade to divorce its scenes from the normal world, and give them a purely subjective significance. Griffith indeed had already developed close-ups and elementary cutting; but the former was familiar in life, though it extended the capabilities of the stage; while the latter, which was confined to scenes of last-minute rescue, where a more and more rapid inter-cutting between hero, heroine and villain heightened the urgency of the situation, did not seem able to be very widely or profoundly applied. It was thus that *Dr. Caligari* became the first film to shock the public out of its acceptance of the cinema as an instrument of realism. Its effect was naturally only limited; but it served to create in later years an atmosphere of sympathy towards the more extreme *surréaliste* productions, and of understanding towards its own successors in Germany, which, removed as they were from pure subjectivism, yet imposed upon natural material a unity of distortion and design.

The great[1] German school of 1920-1925 revived

[1]Great, that is, in relation to other achievements of the cinema. Words of approval in this book must be considerably scaled down if they are to be related to other arts.

the epic tradition of Griffith with such films as *Destiny* and *The Nibelungen Saga* (Fritz Lang, 1921 and 1923); and *The Last Laugh* and *Faust* (F. W. Murnau, 1925 and 1926). The work of this school was marked by slow development and static outlook; the settings in each case displayed dignity, beauty and ample size. A tendency to ponderousness was in the best examples counteracted by significance of theme, which was brought into the closest relation with its environment by the fact that productions were invariably undertaken in the studio, where conditions of lighting and atmosphere, and construction even of natural scenery, were perfectly under control.

It was in these conditions that many of the ablest film actors of to-day[1] received their first training in the cinema. The adventure of a new art, and the limitations of cost which circumstances often imposed, spurred them and the directors who controlled them to the greatest exertions. Their talent impressed even the Hollywood magnates of the day, on whose invitation they visited America, and frequently contracted for a series of films. The atmosphere of wealth and idleness, however, and the commercial outlook of the industry, relaxed their endeavours; a few tricks of the camera impressed the Americans with superior 'art'; but the idealism dis-

[1] *E.g.* Emil Jannings, Werner Krauss and Conrad Veidt.

appeared, and the German school was dissolved. Fritz Lang, who never directed in America, deserted his epics for crime films and fantasies; but his mind, though displaying a great power of imagination and detail, never grasped the principles of film construction—he remains the showman of the cinema.

Ernst Lubitsch turned in Hollywood to light comedy, with an occasional gleam of satire. His versatility has been shown by his readiness to create entertainment out of many passing fancies, but his gifts in this direction are far inferior to René Clair's. Only a single film has indicated that he has the promise of more serious ability.[1] He was highly praised at the time for his prompt and enlightened acceptance of sound; but if this is evidence of the versatility we have mentioned, the fact that his use of sound is the same now as it was five years ago betrays the absence of even this quality from his later work.

F. W. Murnau is the foremost example of the decline which Hollywood brought about; only in his last film before his death,[2] when he was free from its influence, did he return to his former standard. Among actors, Emil Jannings became in America a caricature of his real self; Conrad Veidt has never

[1] *The Man I Killed.*

[2] *Tabu*, a film of the South Sea Islands, made in collaboration with Robert Flaherty.

rivalled his performances in *Caligari* and *The Student of Prague.* So the tradition of the German school was broken; its principal directors and actors were scattered; and the vast productions of Ufa, starting in the direct line with *The Blue Angel*, approximated more and more closely to American methods, and lost every quality of lasting value.

4. In the meantime, however, a new school was developing which, though it has been as much reviled and overpraised as any manifestation of modern art, has advanced steadily along its original lines, and now shows more freedom and originality than ever before. The U.S.S.R. realized from the beginning the powers of persuasion and inspiration which were then no more than latent in the cinema. The Russian task was to convince a forgetful and ignorant mass of peasants of the horrors of the Tsarist régime, and encourage them in the labours which fell to its successors to establish a new community based on justice, and a new social and economic mechanism to repair the ravages of the war. To this end, a school of cinematography was set up. The great Russian directors of to-day played their part in its establishment, and have since helped its development by their teaching; there was no political heresy to divide their loyalties, no competition between firms to impede the free transfer of knowledge and assistance. From the first the Russians

gained ground by their shortage of film, which forced them to abandon diffuse and circuitous methods of narration—then, as they still are, prevalent elsewhere—in favour of a compressed juxtaposition of important details and incidents, which may in life have occurred far apart. The process of film construction on these lines, which grew out of the experiments of Kuleshov in 1922, came to be known as montage,[1] and has since been regarded as supernatural, pretentious and non-existent according to the degree of ignorance or political prejudice affected by the writer.

The two outstanding Russian directors are Eisenstein and Pudovkin. Eisenstein is the chief theorist of the silent cinema, as he is the most powerful practical exponent of the silent film. *The Battleship Potemkin* (1925) revealed the extraordinary energy of a proper combination of shot-subjects and lengths. The commanding power of the battleship was contrasted at first with the submission of the men upon it. Slowly, however, discontent at the disgusting nature of the food, and the overbearing hostility of the officers, gathered into rebellion; the ship was

[1] It has been found convenient to pronounce the word montage in the English manner. Germany already has *montage*, and Italy *montaggio*; and if montage could be firmly established in our language, it might the sooner find a place in future supplements to the *Oxford Dictionary*.

ultimately taken over by the revolutionaries, and piloted into Odessa; and there the crowd, which had been mowed down by Tsarist forces on the harbour steps with pitiless cruelty, was rescued and restored. This film was perhaps the first Soviet work of art to achieve wide recognition outside Russia; everywhere its remarkable force was the subject of discussion and praise; but in England its public exhibition was forbidden by the censor. For many years the Americans had swamped this country with propaganda for their own domestic standards and morals, set forward in films devoid of any vestige of aesthetic value. Yet because they represented a stable and democratic, even if degraded, society, they were considered innocuous; while the Russian films, springing from a renaissance of life which, even if it was misguided or futile, was the historical development of a great people and thus entitled to respect, were denounced as pernicious and banned. The strong presentation of opinion, if acceptable, was called publicity; but if alien, propaganda.

In his subsequent silent films, *The General Line* (1926-1929) and *October* (1927-1928), Eisenstein confirmed the impressions of *Potemkin*. His power of evoking emotion from the simplest material was unparalleled; and to it was later matched the belief that even subtle intellectual concepts could be conveyed by the silent cinema. His last two silent films attempted this task, but it was interrupted by the coming of sound. His first sound film, *Romance Sentimentale* (1931), was the cinema's first successful lyric; while even in the miscellaneous collection of shots purloined from his Mexican epic *Que Viva Mexico*, and entitled *Thunder Over Mexico*, a sense of depth and tragedy was revealed. Of his theories of montage it is not necessary to speak here; they are the basis of the treatment of that subject in Chapter VI. His theories of sound are nowhere very clearly explained or exemplified; *Romance Sentimentale* made evocative use of music, but was not planned on a sufficient scale to afford any generalization of method. Still less *Thunder Over Mexico*, which was accompanied by the musical treacle intended, in British and American films, to prevent audiences from being aroused out of their stupor by any necessarily sudden cessation of speech. Some comment, however, on the internal monologue will be found in Chapter V.

Both Eisenstein and Pudovkin have travelled in their development of style farther and farther from mechanistic methods towards the subjective unity of poetic composition; but whereas in choice of material the former has moved from the ruthless forces of revolution nearer to poetry and human tragedy, the latter has proceeded in the reverse direction. Pudovkin, after an initial essay in physiology entitled

The Mechanics of the Brain (1925), made *Mother* (1926), in which occurred a number of passages of pictorial imagery, after the manner of the simile.[1] His work was already marked by a peculiar ability to reduce the content of a scene to its component terms, selecting the most vital, and synthesizing them in such a way that the whole was conveyed with the utmost economy of means. This was most strikingly evident in his first sound film, *Deserter* (1931-1933), but its beginnings appeared in *Mother, The End of St. Petersburg* and *Storm Over Asia*. These films, no less than Eisenstein's, displayed the utmost concentration in their separate sequences; but to a Western mind they appeared to stray from the main theme without sufficient excuse, like the novels of Tolstoy or even of Dostoievsky. Pudovkin's silent films were conceived less perfectly as independent entities than were Eisenstein's; they frequently demanded the addition of sound, as if Pudovkin was already conceiving the theories which bore such remarkable fruit in *Deserter*.

Inferior only to Eisenstein and Pudovkin is Dovjenko, the director of *Arsenal* (1929) and *Earth* (1930). The former of these films was little seen in this country, owing to its preoccupation with the peculiar and often unintelligible customs of the Ukraine. It is said, however, to have shown remark-

[1]See further pp. 248-250 below.

able promise; and Mr. Paul Rotha prophesied for its
successors a place among the finest Russian films.[1]
Earth was produced just before the U.S.S.R. turned
to sound; and it combines in an exceptional degree a
love of the land and of the simplicity of the peasants
who worked on it, with argument for the coming of
machinery and the destruction of the old life. This
balanced, not to say conflicting, outlook did not commend itself to the Soviet authorities at a time when
the collectivization of farms was at a critical and dangerous juncture. It was evident that external pressure or internal indecision had destroyed the unity
of Dovjenko's work, which remained, however, a
moving if unreconciled account of the Russian
struggle between old and new, against a background
of changeless and unheeding forces. Here in particular was to be observed the narrowing influence of a
control of art vested exclusively in the State, though
no doubt the increasing successes of Communism
in Russia will temper a severity necessary only in a
period of transition. Already the film of Dostoievsky's
life, and the plans for production in 1934-1935, give
promise of freer channels of expression.

These are the left-wing directors; thus named not,
of course, from their place in the political spectrum,
but from their revolt against naturalism and stage
technique. Chief among Russian right-wing directors

[1]*The Film Till Now*, p. 164.

is Alexander Room. His early silent films relied in large measure on the acting ability of his casts, and the main assistance rendered by his camera lay in selecting the gestures and facial expressions which a theatre audience might have overlooked. Apart from this, his technique was straightforward; but his gift of psychological insight made his best-known film, *Bed and Sofa* (1927), a commendable essay in an inferior branch of the cinema. In *The Ghost that Never Returns* (1929), however, he partially adopted left-wing technique, but his use of it was weak and unconvincing. There undoubtedly exists in Russia a place for a director with great ability and simple ideas of presentation. The State cannot ensure that a company of the best actors shall visit each of the innumerable villages of Russia; while orthodox stage technique is easier for the simple-minded to grasp in its essentials than is the complex system of rhythms employed by Eisenstein and Pudovkin.

5. In Germany this task was undertaken by G. W. Pabst. The German school was too rigid in outlook to adapt itself to changing public needs, or build new matter of interest out of current happenings. Pabst, on the other hand, owing much to the teaching of psychology, penetrated into recesses of human character which had seemed inaccessible to the silent film; and beneath the appearance of a superficial and popular story, intended for the common audience,

presented values which only the more sensitive could appreciate. His best silent films were *The Joyless Street* (1925) and *The Loves of Jeanne Ney* (1928). They now appear faded. The remembered films of their time, like *The Battleship Potemkin* or *Le Chapeau de Paille d'Italie*, excelled because either their technique or their theme was exceptionally advanced. But the former of these films would never have been successful outside Russia, and the latter was never successful at all. Pabst had to please a public for whom obviousness had to be carried to the point of burlesque before it was appreciated. Hence the false beards and extravagant gestures of the villains in *The Joyless Street*; and the blue, pink and orange coloured shots which indicated different degrees of debauchery in the homes of those who feasted while Vienna starved. In the street, however, Pabst was more at home, and conveyed something of the hopeless persistence with which the crowds waited for the opening of the butcher's shop. Thus early he began to turn from his preoccupation with the individual to the portrayal of the mass.[1]

6. We must now turn back to the beginnings of film history, in order to trace the development of comedy. Slapstick, as we have seen, gained a great impetus from the cinema, passing during the early

[1]See p. 80 below.

years of the war into the Mack Sennett series of comedies, in which Chaplin first appeared on the screen. It was then the remarkable speed and dexterity of his movements that attracted attention; but in his later films he was able to supplement humour by pathos and even tragedy. The elements of caricature disappeared; Chaplin, always good natured, always disappointed, put up a fight against insuperable difficulties which, by inattention, whimsicality or lack of personal attractiveness, he failed to circumvent. He personified the unsuccessful sides of all who saw him, blending his representations with the humour which never deserted him, and thus sending his audiences away laughing, as they thought, at him, little realizing how for the time their self-pity had been melted by laughing at themselves. In the silent period these qualities were best seen in *The Gold Rush* (1925) and *The Circus* (1927-1928); but they were not fully matured until *City Lights* (1928-1931).

From the standpoint of film technique, Chaplin's work is fairly elementary. His knowledge of gesture and significant detail is indeed outstanding; but his sense of construction, and his placing of the camera, owe little to the special properties of the film.

7. In Europe, Chaplin's work has been extended by a disciple, René Clair. Starting with *Paris Qui*

Dort (1922), which, for all its extravagance and absurdity, anticipated in many ways his subsequent style, he went on to a *dadaiste* film, *Entr'acte* (1923-1924), and thence through various unimportant fantasies to *Le Chapeau de Paille d'Italie* (1928). Here he reached the height of his powers. Hampered by lack of funds, and compelled to use the poorest film stock, which was already in 1931 discoloured, he compressed into every shot a satirical comment on the French *petit bourgeoisie*. The plot was farcical; but farce was never allowed to reduce the satire to absurdity. This film at once became highly unpopular, and Clair was forced for a year to retire from production. *Les Deux Timides*, which followed in 1929, was noted for some ingenious camera tricks, in which the shot was split in half by a vertical division, so that the occupants of each section could be imagined as spatially remote from one another. The hilarious speed of the earlier film was absent, however, and nothing took its place.

Clair has never shown himself a master of the camera; his 'set-ups' are hasty and often ill-considered; but he excels in the fluidity of his action, and the fertility of his ideas. Even in his worst films an occasional shrewd observation reveals a sensitive mind, obscured sometimes by sentimentality and sometimes untrammelled and riotous.

8. Meanwhile in England scarcely any advance

was made in the art of the cinema from 1920-1928. Our own films were feeble imitations of the American; we clamoured for greater resources, but, obtaining them, could only buy the technical improvements of Hollywood. Their films, vulgar as they often were, had force and novelty; ours were vulgar, slow and hackneyed together. Anthony Asquith stands out as the director of the period who seemed most conscious of the marvellous natural material which England offered; but the difficulties of commercial studios, combined with a certain weakness of style, prevented a full realization of these opportunities.

9. In America there was little produced, except by Chaplin, which was remembered for more than a month or two. A single movement, the "Western", showed promise of achievement; *The Covered Wagon* (1923) removed the film from studio artificialities; and its successors, *Cimarron* (1930) and *The Conquerors* (1932), show that documentary value is still appreciated by Americans. In this tradition were the silent films of Flaherty, *Nanook of the North* (1924) and *Moana* (1926); their stories were strictly confined, but they had a unity of theme and presentation; they will be seen when the super-productions are forgotten.

Little effort was made to launch these better films into success; but, to secure an adequate return on the more lavish investments, a new instrument of publicity was devised. The star system is Hollywood's human shop-window. At first the constant intermarriage and divorce of the stars sufficed to excite attention to it; but a tendency to diminishing return indicated a search for fresh novelties. Orgies and purity campaigns were rapidly alternated; a craze for bicycling was succeeded by a craze for maternity; and there was fierce competition to secure a birthplace which would redound to the credit of mother and child alike. To this end, aeroplanes were chartered to hover over San Francisco; and the impetus thus given to the birth of genius was marked by the offer of a long contract in the studios, to take effect immediately. No sooner, however, was an infant thereby made famous, than a racing car tearing round a local track presented a competitor whose even more exceptional entrance into the world gave promise of far greater powers; and so the relentless struggle went on.[1] There were other curious repercussions; the high velocity of marital circulation upset the normal relations; stars were married by telephone, though separated by thousands of miles and by contracts with many years to run; and, on the other hand, they were divorced clasped in one another's arms. If they remarried at once, they tasted

[1] Cf. *Evening Standard*, Oct. 11, 1934: 'The youngest star of them all, though, is baby Phyllis Rica Trey, who was cast for a part in *The Lemon Drop Kid* before she was born.'

a second time the joys of a perfect choice; if they married others, they secured the pleasures of adultery, which had again acquired a scarcity value, now that there was such simplicity of marriage and divorce. It would be a jaded or intelligent world which was not properly impressed by these happenings; but in 1928 the cinema began to lose its hold on the public, and cast round for untried attractions.

It has seemed necessary to trace the history of the film through many branches and countries down to this coming of speech, and then to start again on the succeeding five years; for the transition was marked by a radical change of aim and outlook. The cinema had previously prided itself on its international appeal: commercially, there was much to favour a product which was equally acceptable everywhere, and which incurred no more than costs of distribution as it travelled across the world; aesthetically, there was supposed to be something especially noble in an art which could speak the same message wherever it went, produced by an international mind for an international mind. With speech it was otherwise. Difficulties were indeed clumsily overcome by vast multilingual productions, in which inspiration was crushed by the weight of repetition and the impossibility of the director's attempt to grasp successively the mind of three different nations. This expedient was in consequence abandoned; and the previous cosmopolitan cry was conveniently changed for a eulogy of the national film. The result in this country was a series of all-English productions; Germans, Hungarians, Americans and Frenchmen secured posts as scenario-writers, directors, camera-men, technicians and stars; the floor of the studio was, however, built on English soil. Thus all parties were pleased; patriotism was combined with free exchange; and the film, placed now in the category of salt or sausages, flourished exceedingly.

Of the commercial products of America little need be said. For a short period, when the mere sound of the voice was miraculous, there was a close adherence to the stage, both in style and subject. Subsequently, however, Hollywood decided to exploit the sensations of the moment, and developed a new technique of rapid changes of scene, and dialogue packed with humour and meaning. Of this type, *The Front Page* (Milestone, 1932) is still the outstanding example, though it was shown in England more than two years ago; for ruthless energy, perfect precision of timing and exquisite continuity, no film of any country other than Russia has challenged it.

10. America has on many occasions dared to fail. *Strange Interlude*, with its curious spoken thoughts, together with the experiments in 'narratage', have

been bold attempts in the evolution of new technique. The rate of production necessary to cover studio expenses has, however, militated against prolonged research. If a new idea succeeds at once, it is adopted; if not, it is rejected without further trial.

But if a consistently high level is beyond hope as the industry is now constituted, so too is there little danger of the best American films falling as low as the best British. The American director knows what he wants to do, and does it; if his film is to be a screen-play, he withdraws attention from his medium and concentrates it on the personality of his characters[1]; if it is to be a true film, he can command every resource of the camera to make it more graphic and convincing. Thus *The Conquerors* made use of artificial visual similes and optical distortions to convey those general conceptions of the American stock-market boom, crash and slump which the characters of the film could not vividly enough represent.

Hitherto Hollywood propaganda has been of a double-edged type. The war films seemed to half the audience a glorification of war, and to the other half an exposure of its futility. Many of the gangster films encouraged sympathy with the gangsters, while at the same time revealing the pernicious

[1] E.g. *The Barretts of Wimpole Street* (Franklin, 1934), *Men in White* (Boleslavsky, 1934).

effects which they exercised on American life. Some even of the unemployment films (e.g. *Gold Diggers of 1933*) were at once a mockery of poverty in presenting it amid the glitter of the music-hall stage, and a revelation of it in presenting it at all in such circumstances. Thus the good effects of social indignation were half wasted by being blended with sensation. The recent depression, however, has woken Hollywood to some recognition of the deeper conflicts of life; and the best American films are now inspired with much sincerity of purpose (e.g. *Zoo in Budapest* (Lee, 1933), except the last reel; *Three Cornered Moon* (Nugent, 1933); *Emperor Jones* (Murphy, 1933)).

In one respect the influence of American films has been wholly good, and above the competition of all other countries. Walt Disney started his synchronized cartoons in 1929, and mounted steadily from the cinema's comic poet to become its singer of lyrics and teller of fairy tales. The adventures of his famous Mickey Mouse, the dog Pluto and the other animals have the inconsequence and incongruity which are the delight of children. It is not the happiness of the good princess or the final wretchedness of her captors which attracts them, nor the melancholy fates which overtook the characters of *Struwwelpeter* for their bad behaviour, but the freakishness of the poetic world, the goblins and fairies, the boy sailing behind his umbrella into the skies. Children find themselves hampered by parental restrictions from following their imaginations out of their ordinary lives. Only fantasy, whether of word or picture, gives them this freedom; and to-day the Disney film, with the vividness of life and the strangeness of fairyland, is ready to carry them away. In particular, animals have been brought closer to men; their plots, loves, dreams and rescues may not recommend themselves to reason and Pavlov; but Disney invests them, as did Kenneth Grahame in *The Wind in the Willows*, with a half-humanity more like themselves for being more like us. Anthropomorphism may be the bane of scientist and theologian, but it is part of the poet's equipment.

Passing to the English commercial cinema (we shall refer to the work of special groups later), there is little of interest to record. We have several competent directors, who are given poor material to work on, and as a rule handle it poorly. An occasional exception in the latter respect (e.g. *The Private Life of Henry VIII* (Korda, 1933)) is greeted with extravagant praise; this film owed nothing of value to the cinema; and the fact that it was actually not adapted from a play served only to show that it would be better adapted into one. Our own industry is financially more flourishing than the American; and our film producers have in consequence lapsed into complacent satisfaction, grinding out stage substitutes in the knowledge that anything British and boosted will be acclaimed by critics and public alike.

11. The first years of the German sound cinema were marked by Pabst's three best films. *Westfront 1918* (1930) showed the comradeship as well as the futility of war; *Die Dreigroschen Oper* (1931) translated the German version of Gay's famous opera on to the screen; and *Kameradschaft* (1932) illustrated from a pre-war mining disaster on the Franco-German frontier the cessation of hostility which an impersonal and inevitable catastrophe can accomplish; and it pleaded for such a common front between the two nations to-day against the dangers which threatened them both. Pabst's use of sound was masterly; it was naturalistic, in that he did not suppress natural sounds which would be expected to be heard (in this differing from Pudovkin); while he arranged that only those sounds were produced which contributed to the heightening of the desired effect; and contrapuntal, in that sounds were not necessarily matched with a record of their sources. It is impossible to forget the slow, gigantic crescendo of the final French advance in *Westfront*, when the increasing battery of fire and the creeping progress of the tanks annihilated the German troops and among them the friends who had been heroes of the film.

In these three films Pabst displayed a remarkable

sense of camera-angle, which he was able to maintain even when his camera was constantly moving. The Russian directors rely very largely on the still camera, and thereby keep pictorial composition under more precise control. Cutting also is freer, in that movement of the camera in relation to the material, or material travelling past the camera, partly dictates its own rate of cutting and impedes construction from the shots of an independent rhythm. Pabst's work, therefore, inclined to imperceptible cutting, in which the eye is induced in any one shot, whether by movement or distance of the main subject, to anticipate those qualities in its successor. By this process the spectator's mind is guided here and there, passing by swift and smooth transitions from one incident to another, following the director in the unfolding of his theme. This method of absorption is radically different from that demanded by left-wing directors.[1]

Since *Kameradschaft*, Pabst has seemed ill at ease. *L'Atlantide* (1932) and *Don Quixote* (1933) dealt with individuals by objective methods which had proved appropriate to his mass films, but here did not pierce below the superficial layers of character. He is now in Hollywood; but it is hoped that he is not going the way of all German directors who have hitherto worked there. At present the German cine-

[1]See Chapters V and VI below.

ma is in a state of transition. Having purged it of all non-Aryan influences, the rulers of Germany have found that there is nothing good left in it. They have therefore set themselves to build up a new cinema, foreseeing that, though adulation is all that is now demanded of propaganda, the time will come when the most powerful persuasion will be needed.

12. The cinema in France is considered by French writers to be moribund. The majority of films there are certainly flat and lifeless, having succumbed to the imitation of foreign methods. Judged by these standards, however, the critic in every country (not excluding Russia) would despair. It is only possible to select a few outstanding films from an immense output for even the most guarded praise. France, though she may have a low average, has a high standard of exceptions. René Clair's two sentimental comedies, *Sous les Toits de Paris* (1930) and *Le Quatorze Juillet* (1933), and his two mixtures of burlesque and satire, *Le Million* (1931) and *A Nous la Liberté* (1932), are the gayest and freest films that have been made. His songs, his choruses and his commentative music emancipate the action from the plodding rhythms of conversational speech. He lives in a borderland world between fact and fancy, and when the voice of Signor Sopranelli causes a candelabra to shiver and tinkle, or when the missing coat in *Le Million* passes from hand to hand as it is

chased with a dull thud, and finally becomes a foot-
ball and is struggled for in a scrum, no violence
seems to be done to the demands of naturalism.
René Clair's films are not popular in France, but are
so essentially French that it is hoped he will not try,
as he is reported to be proposing, to capture the
idiom of the English life.

The second most noteworthy branch of the French
cinema is the psychological film. French camera-
work has always excelled in an intimate quality,
searching out the small important details of a scene,
and establishing contact between the characters and
the spectators. In many cases the result has been no
more than a very competent screen-play; but sometimes a real love of the open air, combined with a
knowledge of the true resources of the cinema, has
produced a memorable sequence. This occurred in
La Maternelle (Benoit-Levy and Marie Epstein,
1933), a study of childhood, which came alive in a
way owing nothing to the stage, in the sequence of
the girl's attempted suicide.

13. The Russians were well aware that their resources would only allow a very retarded approach
to the sound cinema. It was foolish to make sound
films (which soon became possible) so long as they
could not be exhibited in the small remote cinemas
for whose frequenters they were intended. Three of
the greatest Russian directors, therefore, Pudovkin,

Eisenstein and Alexandrov (the last being Eisenstein's assistant), issued a statement which was published in *Close-Up* in October 1928. They prophesied with considerable accuracy the stages which the 'talkie' was to go through, and concluded by saying that speech, though it would in most respects be a drag on the development of the cinema, would resolve many of the difficulties of explanation which the silent film had increasingly met with as its themes became more complicated (*October* had more than 300 titles in a length of two and a half hours). The first Russian sound films were not very promising. *Alone* (Trauberg, 1931) was slow and uninspired; *The Road to Life* (Ekk, 1931), though it had one or two good musical sequences, was not far ahead of Western films in sound technique. It was, however, the first Russian film to achieve commercial success in England and the U.S.A. Its story, of the recovery and disciplining of wild boys, was as faultless as a religious tract; its types were a little uncouth, but then, of course, they were Russians, and that was different.

It was not until *Deserter* (Pudovkin, 1931-1933) that the Russian sound film came into its own, and established a lead over other countries at least as great as in the silent cinema. We shall refer so frequently to *Deserter* in the following pages that only a little need be said of it here. A theme which was too academic for the cinema slowed its development somewhat: a revolutionary worker in Hamburg gave up his task for a safe position in Russia, but was ultimately persuaded by his conscience and the death of a friend in Germany to return there to the struggle. Into this framework a great number of ideas were fitted. The different attitudes of various grades of socialism to the strike-weapon; the psychology of picketing, and the gradual weakening of the old men in the face of starvation; the stubborn resistance of the women to concessions; the desperation and suicide of some of the workers, and the good humour which saved the others; the relentless counterattacks of capitalism when its supremacy was threatened; the servile complacency of the police in the sufferings of the strikers; these views, although of course biassed, were presented with a force and sympathy which commanded respect even from the non-socialist. But the portraits of the capitalists themselves were only slightly less exaggerated than those of ten years ago. They lolled listlessly in expensive cars, or slouched in restaurants, blandly ignoring the disappointments and deaths of the strikers. As a caricature, they were amusing enough; but in a serious and even scathing denunciation of the capitalist system, they were altogether out of place.

In technique *Deserter* was far ahead of any film yet produced. The amount of time and care which had gone to its making was evidently very great;

but it was shot through by an inspiration which lightened the burden of the film and gave it speed and urgency. Its effect was certainly more powerful than that of any film which had preceded it, not only in respect of tension and excitement (whose production Eisenstein had mastered many years before), but in depth and universality of suffering.

14. One more strand of film history has to be followed up. Since 1920, with *The Cabinet of Dr. Caligari*, there had existed in many countries a so-called *advance-guard* cinema, pledged to the development of the art without restriction from commercial interests. Often degenerating into artiness, or becoming the slave of a school of painters, it yet widened considerably an understanding of the medium. Thus in 1925 Cavalcanti in *Rien que les Heures* was using the wipe with intelligence and restraint, and was exploring the *surréaliste* methods of free mental association of images. Deslaw's *La Marche des Machines* and the abstract sequences in *Metropolis* showed the possibilities of extracting pure compositions from machinery, which have since become the commonplace of advanced commercial directors when they have wished to express 'the spirit of industry'. A return to formalism in machinery was made recently by Professor Moholy-Nagy in *Lichtspiel*, in which revolving spirals and balls running up and down grooves succeeded one another in intentionally

meaningless patterns. A part of this film is accessible as a prelude to Stuart Legg's telephone film, *The Coming of the Dial*.

The most notable *surréaliste* films have been *Le Chien Andalou* (Bunuel), *The Sea-Shell and the Clergyman* (Dulac, 1929) and *Le Sang d'un Poète* (Cocteau, 1932). It is almost impossible to criticize these films. '*Surréalisme* . . . demands a completely free and unbiassed play of thought. The appearance of unusual images of any kind should not, therefore, be questioned. More than this. The perfect *surréaliste* film should not even arouse any emotions which would make the onlooker question anything in it. The images, the symbols, should demand acceptance, as they surely would if they were genuine. That is where *Le Sang d'un Poète* is perfect. The film is almost hypnotic . . . (it is) the real representation of dream—of unbiassed thought, free from all aesthetic and moral preoccupations.'[1] The adherents of this movement are easily hypnotized into suspending their critical faculty; others, to whom the succession of images often seems childish or demented, are critical and so debarred from relevant criticism.

15. But a tendency to exaggerate in the cinema must never be deplored. There is so little inventive activity at work that advance almost always comes in

[1] From a review of *Le Sang d'un Poète* ; *film*, spring 1933, p. 15.

the first place from the advance-guard; while the younger directors often grow milder with experience, and turn to the making of straightforward documentaries. England's only solid contribution to the cinema lies in her documentary groups, and in particular the G.P.O. Film Unit, which now carries on the activities of a department of the defunct Empire Marketing Board. With the production of John Grierson's *Drifters* (1929) a tradition was founded of interesting, and in the widest sense educating, the public in the business of community life. Following the wise policy initiated by Sir Stephen Tallents,[1] a group was started under the auspices of the E.M.B. to give publicity to domestic and imperial government enterprise. Mr. Grierson was at its head, and was responsible for the training of its directors and the production of its films. Production in this unit is co-operative: that is to say, a great part of its personnel is engaged upon each stage, preparing the script, shooting the material and cutting sight and sound to make the final film. Thus Mr. Grierson's work informs not only each production, but every part of each; and it is much more misleading in this unit to credit the director with the whole excellence of a good film than in the majority of the instances hitherto discussed. The example of Soviet Russia has been followed in making the director *primus inter*

[1] See *The Projection of England.*

pares, a leader among colleagues instead of a personality dominating the actions of a number of assistants. With these provisos in mind, it will be convenient to describe the work of the unit under the heads of its several directors, whose individual styles, no less than Mr. Grierson's, are distinctly recognizable in its productions. The volume of output, together with the present difficulty of seeing these films, prohibits reference to more than a few representative examples, which have been selected because of their comparatively wide exhibition in commercial cinemas.

Paul Rotha, a former member of the unit, has made three important films, *Contact*, *Roadwards*, and *Rising Tide*. While his sense of pictorial values and knowledge of cutting have steadily improved, they have not been brought to bear on the social and industrial problems which form the main theme of his films. He tries to give instruction by a method which is purely emotional, and is thus in danger of losing the way between two of the aims of documentary—education and impression.

In this respect Rotha exhibits more clearly than do other G.P.O. directors a fault which weakens the work of the whole unit, and indeed of all that branch of art which, like the Soviet, professes only to value sociological effect. Lyrical elements, in that event, can only be excused as a concession to the natural folly of directors, or explained as a sugar coating of emotion needed to induce the public to swallow an intellectual pill. If the last reel of *Aero-Engine*, the last sequence of *Weather Forecast* and the opening of the cable in *Under the City* are felt to be harmonious lyrical elements in the informative structure of these films, then aesthetic theory must not dispute and can only attempt to rationalize them. But if these elements appear intrusive, the theory on which documentary films are based must be reconstructed and more clearly stated, so that further incongruities may be avoided.

Stuart Legg has made several telephone films, the most important of which are *Telephone Workers* and *The Coming of the Dial*, and *The Voice of Britain*, an ambitious documentary on the B.B.C. His work is marked by a scrupulous attention to camera-angle, which, when it does not wholly fix the mind on qualities of pure design, conveys a very precise and powerful sense of atmosphere. It leads also to a concentration on static effects which might not appeal to a public educated in the rush and movement of the American cinema. Legg has experimented successfully with speech which, starting from an alliance with the speaker, continues over a divergent picture and imparts a greater openness as well as a greater contrastive force to a basically orthodox system of dialogue.

90

The Song of Ceylon

Basil Wright has steadily tended away from information to emotion and atmosphere. His earlier films, *The Country Comes to Town* and *O'er Hill and Dale*, were spoilt by commentaries added by another firm. In their original silent form, however, they explained in conceptual terms the nature of the subject he was treating. Indeed he proved outstandingly successful in communicating ideas without the use of speech or titles. In course of time his subjects became simpler and simpler, culminating in his longest film, *The Song of Ceylon*. Here he was content to ignore the multiplicity of religions in Ceylon, the relations between the various races and the economic life of the country, the processes involved in the manufacture of tea and other commodities. What he did dwell on he impressed with outstanding force. The deep veneration, alternated with ecstatic fervour, with which the Buddha is still worshipped was set against the jangle and modern clamour of Colombo—the handicrafts, honourably maintained for centuries even by the aristocratic Singalese, against the mechanized labour carried on in the factories by Tamils. But the dialectic presentation of these ideas admitted of conflicting conclusions. Some thought that Wright was denouncing the imposition of capitalist industry on a people fitted only for the slow dignity of crafts and the worship of a wholly Oriental religion. Others thought that he was commending the benefits brought by British influence to bear upon an antiquated and outworn culture.

This film, which was in any event of the greatest significance and beauty, has not yet been publicly shown in its original form, except to the Film Society.

Arthur Elton's films are mainly devoted to the subject of industry in relation to the worker and the public. In *The Voice of the World* he dealt with the effect of radio on national life, the factory sections giving an impressionistic rather than a descriptive account of the building of radio sets. *Aero-Engine*, on the other hand, proved that accuracy of treatment was by no means incompatible with beauty of photography and cutting.

R. H. Watt has made three films, of which the first, *6.30 Collection*, was notable for its use of random dialogue and natural sound to give atmospheric effect. It was deliberately pitched in a low key, and was thus a refreshing contrast to the hysterical over-statement which mars a large section of the cinema to-day. *Droitwich* is valuable as a faithful as well as an imaginative record of the construction of a giant broadcasting station, from the choice of the site to the issue of the first programme.

Evelyn Spice directed *Weather Forecast*, which became the most famous of the 1934 group of G.P.O. films. It had a well-defined central theme, the pre-

Factors Governing Film Production

diction and eventual onset of a storm, round which
the accessory phenomena of meteorology, tele-
graphy and telephony were most ingeniously
grouped. Miss Spice was also responsible for *Spring
on the Farm*, a rather naive essay in bucolic lyricism,
accompanied by a musical pastiche of harpsichord
and folk music.

16. The commercial film of to-day is the result of
the interaction of personal and economic factors.
During the boom period of 1920-1929 the demand
for entertainment led to an increase in the size and
stupidity of the spectacles presented to the public;
while this tendency towards a lowest common denominator greatly extended the numbers of the film
audience, the receipts of the industry, and so the
gratification of the original demand. In practice,
therefore, productions steadily grew larger and more
senseless. Film magnates, wishing to extend their
profits, had to broaden the basis of their appeal.
Lower and lower levels of intelligence were drawn
into the cinemas; the same films were supposed to
satisfy every type of audience; and hence the general
taste became increasingly depraved. This interpretation of the facts is confirmed by the reversal of the
last three years.[1] During the slump the level of
incomes dwindled, the demand for cinema entertain-

[1]The trend of development was upset from 1929-1931 by
the advent and establishment of sound.

ment was found to be more elastic than film magnates had anticipated, and attendance rapidly declined. The consequent decrease in the scale of individual productions gave greater opportunity to the real talent which the industry had attracted but hitherto crushed; and there resulted a considerable improvement in the standard of films, which was accepted by uncritical *habitués* and appreciated by true admirers of the cinema. The average standard of films and audiences was in consequence equated again at a higher, though less remunerative, level.

These facts seem to indicate that intelligence is either dispersed more or less equally throughout the income-groups, or is concentrated to some extent towards the upper end; for, if the contrary were the case, the dwindling of audiences would have lowered the average standard (the poorest and most intelligent being forced to withdraw), and the observed raising of the standard, which no film magnate would have provided gratuitously, would not have taken place.[1] There is still some presumption, however, which is reinforced by the tactics of the film industry during the boom, that intelligence is evenly distributed but poorly represented in film audiences. The Board of Film Censors in England, and the Board of Review in America, are endeavouring to

[1]But in so far as the greater part of the decline occurred in the more expensive seats, this argument would be weakened.

improve the standard of films, but their pronounce-
ments and prohibitions have hitherto been directed to
pacifying by mere evasion the puritanical elements
in the public, rather than to pursuing the often conflicting ideal of artistic excellence. In practice, therefore, the film industry is almost wholly guided by
profit-making motives; and, in so far as this is the
case, the impending economic revival will, on the
considerations discussed, lower once again the standard of commercial films.

Permanent improvement, therefore, if possible at
all, is to be looked for where profit-making is only a
secondary issue. The government films are in England the most important examples of the type, and it
is on this account that the work of the G.P.O. Unit is
of outstanding interest. But because the determining
factor in production is no longer financial, it is not on
that account personal. Novels, paintings, musical
compositions, though to some extent guided by popular taste, are very largely governed by the pre-
dilections of the artist. The majority will approve
and harmonize with the existing social structure; but
small groups, often very disintegrating in the long
run, will exert a revolutionary influence. In the
cinema this is not so; the expensiveness of the medium harnesses it to commercial and political major-
ities. Thus the outlook of the G.P.O. Unit is that of
the government in power. An example may be

given from Stuart Legg's *Telephone Workers*. This film was designed to show the social mechanism of telephone installation. Fields were supplanted by villages, villages by towns; communication at once became essential, engineers planned the telephone system, workers laid out its complicated scheme, and finally co-operation combined with brisk efficiency maintained the network of instruments, lines, charges, checkings and staff. In this film unreserved approval was expressed of the methods of the G.P.O.; but it would not have mattered if attention had been drawn to alleged defects of the system, the incompetence of country services or unjust additions to telephone accounts. In either case the telephone system would have been estimated (as in fact it was) as part of an uncriticized social structure. But had *Telephone Workers* been a socialist attack, it would have diverged far more fundamentally from the actual film than a mere exposure of existing inefficiencies. It would have alleged that those who make telephones are economically debarred from using them, while those who do use them are often idle *rentiers*; and that (though the allegation and the conclusion drawn from it are no doubt false), the Postmaster General is influenced in extending the system rather by the fact that he has large blocks of shares in telephone manufacturing companies than by any concern for those who may benefit by the new service;

and that therefore, as soon as these motives conflict, the individual will gain at the expense of the community.

Thus, even if the laws of libel could be successfully evaded, the making of a film on these lines would be economically impossible under a capitalist government, just as a film advocating the extension of private enterprise would be impossible under a socialist government. Where political issues are concerned, and to-day they penetrate into almost every part of the life of society, the film, unlike the speech, the tract or the novel, is deprived of independence. But where all parties are agreed about the end to be achieved—as, for instance, the spread of education and the abolition of slums—but differ about the ways of reaching it, the cinema has the opportunity of advocating contending views. It is in this field, therefore, that the social influence of the film is likely to be most enduringly felt, since it will here awake the public into independent thought instead of herding it into a mass acquiescence in the existing order.

A separate issue emerges in respect of the personal film, or film with a predominatingly individual appeal. Its production will be governed by the profit-making motives whose results have already been considered; and as no strong autonomous effort towards improvement is likely to come from either party to the exchange, the standard will probably remain low. Yet it might be the case at the same time, that minor and localized influences encouraged the production of exceptions of outstanding merit; and these, having psychological repercussions on film audiences, would exert a pressure on the economics of supply and so raise the standard. The two considerations which to-day mainly govern this issue operate in contrary directions and, being of approximately equal weight, appear to cancel one another out. In the first place, the growth of specialized cinemas catering for a more intelligent demand in this and other countries has recently made possible the production of comparatively cheap films which will meet this demand. And as such cinemas are to-day being started in a number of the less philistine provincial towns, it might be expected that a large marginal audience—which has hitherto only just been persuaded into the ordinary cinemas—would detach itself for the superior interest to be found in these. Since good films, though far too expensive to be undertaken without guarantees of fairly extensive distribution, can often still be made for a tenth or twentieth of the sum necessary to attract the full cinema public, it might seem that equilibrium could be easily established with a moderate financial outlay on production, a reward at the normal rate of interest, and a product of considerable artistic merit.

Here, however, the second factor comes into play. We have seen that political, economic and artistic influences allow as a rule a leavening of the whole output by improved films; that, in fact, the political influence remains neutral, while the economics of supply and the demand for art and entertainment strike a balance at higher and lower levels of excellence. To-day, however, the sphere in which interaction takes place in this way is being rapidly contracted. In totalitarian states, politics, economics and art are chained together to drag the minds of the people remorselessly in one direction. The previous analysis is inapplicable, the possibility of making personal films is extinguished, and the material of the specialized cinemas disappears. This is happening to-day. Apart from revivals, and the importation of old continental films which have not hitherto been seen here, the long films exhibited in these cinemas are almost wholly French. Russia, Italy, Germany, Austria are appealing through the cinema to a sentiment which scarcely exists in this country, and which, if it did exist, would be officially disapproved. Almost every Soviet film has been banned; *Camicia Nera*, a film which celebrated the tenth anniversary of Fascism, has never been commercially exhibited; and the Nazi films, if by some inconceivable accident they were permitted by the censor to be shown, are too dull to gain the attention of the public. England

and America have failed to make better films intentionally appealing to better, and therefore smaller,
audiences; and many of the remaining French films
are too poor to merit exhibition without the backing
of the magic epithet 'Continental'.

Until the film is cheapened, therefore, its future
will lie with its powers as a social instrument. It will
be art if government influences its schools in the appreciation of art, and maintains a high standard in
its own productions; and mob propaganda if political
pressure is brought to bear at once on the great body
of degraded taste. The English documentary movement has taken the first step in the right direction.
But the influence of competition and private enterprise upon the cinema is very strong. Government
productions which appeal to the public by entertainment, as well as instructing it by the force of fact, are
immediately suspect to the trade. The catastrophe
which overtook the French advance-guard movement demonstrated the necessity of combining every
stage of production in the hands of those who are determined to continue it. If the film is conceived by
others, its purpose may be warped; if executed by
others, financial support may be withdrawn; if distributed by others, a boycott may be applied or publicity refused. But it is by no means impossible to
break away from these impediments and set up a
chain stretching from producer to exhibitor. Indeed

this is the only way to overcome the obstructions of the trade, and prove that there is a section of the public better able to appreciate what is good in the cinema than those who cater for its tastes will allow. There is already in this country the nucleus of a cinema which has imagination, social consciousness and the courage to experiment. If the government will still further assist its growth and independence, the public will respond with a keener and more intelligent interest in the government. Films which are able to popularize the dull and sometimes ridiculed processes of administration are worthy of much official encouragement.

Chapter IV

Categories of the Film:
a. Distinctions

'In our most theoretical moods we may be nearest to our most
practical applications.'
WHITEHEAD: *Introduction to Mathematics*

---

1. *The method of investigation involves a considerable
recourse to abstraction.* 2. *The relation of cinema to
stage.* 3. *The film based on their similarity.* 4. *The
film based on their difference.* 5. *The abandonment of
drama.* 6. *The film based on the cinema's independent properties, but borrowing where necessary from
other arts, which is the subject of Chapters V and VI.*

---

1. We can now sum up those conclusions of the
historical sketch which bear on the discussion of film technique to which we next proceed. The
cinema has been too widely exploited by commercial
interests to have followed a healthy line of development; it is too expensive to allow any considerable
leavening of the whole output by small, independent
directors. Only by careful search can any body of films
be got together to form material for an empirical
study of the cinema; and even then they will prove

so inaccessible to the reader that investigation must be preceded by lengthy description. It is possible to mention forty or fifty paintings and pieces of music familiar to anyone in the least likely to take up a serious book on either of those subjects; art galleries and reproductions in the one case, and scores and gramophone records in the other, are at hand to help the memory. But the cinema has no such basis of common appeal; and the writer must in consequence pursue an eclectic course, scattering his references in the hope that a few will escape the stony ground of ignorance. Recourse to abstraction is inevitable in these circumstances. It enables simplified and exactly appropriate examples to be constructed in illustration of particular aspects of the subject. It also focuses attention on fundamental principles. Many people have believed the star system or the stage to be the basis of the cinema; few have recognized it to be montage and the use of differentiating factors. Furthermore, abstraction assists at all stages the recognition of elements previously concealed in the undifferentiated mass; and this, as was indicated in Chapter I, is one of the chief methods by which reasoning furthers aesthetic appreciation. 'Abstraction indeed is not so much the picking out of one element already recognized from a number of others already recognized, but is usually a process in which the abstracted element is for the

103

first time coming into clear consciousness. This process is often slow and the recognition of the true universal grows clearer and clearer as our experience itself grows or as the science which is concerned itself progresses. The act of abstraction then, even when we have the right matter to abstract from, may be difficult.'[1] This, then, is a process which, however difficult, the reader must follow stage by stage for himself; he can no more increase his appreciation of art by learning the conclusions of aesthetics than he can master mathematical thinking by learning the conclusions of mathematical theorems. But abstraction must be brought to earth as often as it can give results of practical value; it must not be pursued for its own sake. This end is best, though of course restrictedly, achieved on the plane of literary criticism, by mentally emending existing films according to the principles which emerge in the course of study; and by relating the cinema to the older and better-established arts.

2. The commercial cinema owes a large and obvious debt to the stage as the source of many of its finest actors, and lately of the greater part of its material. The slavish admiration of the sound film has now many times repaid this debt, whole plays and even whole casts having been transferred almost direct from stage to screen. It is not denied that this

[1]Cook Wilson, *Statement and Inference*, p. 28.

transference fulfils a useful purpose; there are many who cannot, for financial or geographical reasons, see good plays well acted, but who may enjoy their substitutes on the screen. Nor is it denied that the making of screen-plays is an art, as the making of photoplays cannot be, for it involves the discovery of a technique based on a choice of processes, by which the limitations of the cinema in competition with the stage may be reduced or avoided. What is denied is that the screen-play can ever equal or excel the play which it reproduces. It is based on similarities between stage and cinema; if no differences divided them, the screen-play could still only approach to a finite ideal, that of exact reproduction of effect. And as it is, setting aside differences such as colour and solidity which science may nullify in the future, there remains a further difference, as yet not understood and therefore irremediable, but constituting an essential asset of the stage. This is *personality*. Between actor and audience there exists a living link. Both are contained by the same walls. The spectator feels a contact established between himself and the actor, and knows him to be more than can be seen and heard, more than an automaton moving and speaking with supreme skill; something indeed that is vital and immediate—a personality. The actor, on his side, senses, rather than sees or hears, his audience, and is as responsive to the silent disapproval of a small and invisible part of it as to the shouted praise of the majority. That science offers no evidence of this contact is no proof that it does not exist. Emotions, moral values, religious experience, consciousness itself, are accepted as established facts, though science is unaware of them. If personality, as something transmitted with visual contact but essentially different from it, is believed on the evidence of its emotional effect to exist, its scientific obscurity must not be allowed to prejudice this belief. But if personality is accepted as it has been described, its total absence from the cinema must be admitted. The actor projected on a flat screen is a mere bodiless shadow, and an automaton, if its movements could be made sufficiently subtle and flexible, might replace him without the slightest loss of effect.

It is indeed evident that much of what is commonly called personality is in fact conveyed from the film actor to the audience; whatever relies solely on sense-data can, theoretically at least, be recorded and reproduced without loss. The term has, however, been used here to embrace the residuum of personality which lies outside the popular definition. That such a residuum exists is further shown by the inferiority in practice of the screen-play to the play itself. Unless filmic precautions are taken to remedy its natural defects, the screen-play falls into a mere **catalogue** of details, and the spectator inevitably

106

fails to identify himself fully with the feelings of characters possessed of a much less than human 'aliveness'. The power of sympathy depends less on the visible signs of presence than on the mysterious contact of personality.

3. The limiting case of the photo-play makes no attempt to avert this disastrous weakness. It is in the narrowest sense a craft, its sole object being to transfer, in space and time, the point of observation of a true art-form. Thus the gramophone record transfers a piece of music from the listening-point of the best situated among the audience in a hall to some person who may be spatially or temporally remote from it.[1] So the photo-play, from a fixed camera angle and position, reproduces a stage play as exactly as it can; most of its present omissions are due to deficiencies of scientific knowledge, but—which is perhaps outside the range of science—it also omits personality.

The screen-play, on the other hand, tries to rival its stage prototype by conveying so much more of the personality that is seen as to make good the loss of the rest that is sensed. If it must remain content with being a catalogue, it will at least be full and varied.

[1]But in so far as recording is electrically imperfect, and balance and control are used to modify the range of volume and frequency, an element of choice enters in, and the process contains some characteristics of art.

The spatial close-up is the usual means of revealing significant detail and motion. Small movements which must necessarily have escaped the audience of a play sitting removed some distance from its actors can thus be selected from their surroundings and magnified to any extent. On the stage, the most skilled and careful staging cannot ensure that the characters are always seen to the best advantage by any one of the audience; and the whole audience, widely spaced out, has to be considered. The camera is concerned with only a single viewpoint; its position can be altered from moment to moment to fulfil the immediate needs of the action. By exploiting these two advantages—ability to select and magnify, and freedom from limitation of view—the exponents of the screen-play hope to rival the products of the stage. But it cannot be said that they have made the most of this opportunity. Emil Jannings is perhaps the only actor who has been so closely studied that his personality in each new part can be built up in catalogue detail by detail. Everywhere else chances have been thrown away by substituting for this hard task some facile and worthless evasion. Sex-appeal can fortunately be conveyed without troublesome difficulties; and if an actor has gained a reputation on the stage, his name can well replace his personality.

The full force of the stage play is only realized

when its action is concentrated within a narrow space and time. Close interplay of character and motive relies largely for its effect on that personality which, as we have seen, the cinema cannot convey. Thus, those plays which are best on the stage will be least good as films of the type just described; while if the film is good, it must be based on, and show clear signs of, a poor play. A union of stage and film, as in the screen-play, can never be fruitful; each partner will only gain at the expense of the other, and the result will be a vacillating compromise.

4. Thus the attempt to base a true technique of the film on similarities between stage and cinema has failed. The two categories so far discussed, the photo-play and the screen-play, have been shown in theory and practice to be greatly inferior to their prototypes. On the other hand, a film technique which is based solely on differences between stage and cinema is no less likely to fail. To constitute such a 'difference-film' it is not sufficient merely to photograph mountains and streams which are inaccessible to the theatrical producer; the film must choose a method of carrying on its purposive theme or meaning from moment to moment. If it does this by the uninterrupted flux of speech and movement, it is no better than the screen-play or photo-play; if it compromises and achieves its purpose partly by rela-

tional cutting,[1] the film will resemble the stage in the other factor to the compromise; and if, lastly, the relational method is used throughout, and human beings introduced, the film and the stage will still be at one in their pictorial transcription of such beings, living and acting in a three-dimensional space, not pinned down to a moment, as in sculpture or painting, nor removed altogether from the sphere of pictorial art, as in literature.

Thus the only remaining fields for the cinema will be, first, the film of natural objects, whose shots are connected solely by relational cutting (*Romance Sentimentale* and *Brumes d'Automne* are perhaps the closest, though nevertheless very imperfect, examples). Such a film may, of course, describe human emotional states if it does so by selecting and relating material things as they would be seen by the subject of these states. Secondly, the abstract film, portraying moving lines, geometrical figures and other means of exciting pure aesthetic emotion. The brothers Fischinger have produced the best examples of one main class of abstract film. They attempt to illustrate a specially composed sound factor by moving shapes in the visual film. Lately, however (*Lichtertanz, Op. 12*), they seem to rely for their effect on the beauty of the visual film, using the sound factor chiefly as a means of continuity from

[1]See p. 47 above, def. A. *c*. 1.

one shape to another. It is possible that some abstract form as satisfying as musical expression may eventually be evolved. Present examples, however, seem to labour for their very existence, and the sound factor, if it exists, is nearly always of greater interest than the visual film.

It will be seen that the scope of this 'difference-film' is extremely limited, and that its products tend to a sterile intellectuality. If, then, the cinema is to escape a servile and inferior transcription of the stage, or a remoteness from pictured and described humanity which yet cannot touch the heights of musical expression, there are two main courses it can follow: it may either abandon the dramatic altogether, or else explore to their fullest extent its own peculiar properties, accepting from the other arts whatever helps it to achieve this end.

5. The first course embraces the news-reel and the lecture film, whose aim is to record events as they happen, for the purpose of information or instruction. The form of the news-reel is usually the outcome of necessity. The best angle and position for the camera can seldom be secured, or the best type and intensity of lighting. Limitations are certainly the making of an art, but too many limitations can crush it. In these circumstances, the news-reel, despite recent improvements, can hardly be called an art-form, except perhaps of the lowest kind. The lecture-film,

on the other hand, gathers its material over a wide field and can subject it to nearly all the artificial processes which were previously defined. A large amount of skill can therefore go to its making, and, as in some examples of the *Secrets of Nature* series, it may bring the excitement, if not of dramatic effect, at least of vividly acquired knowledge.

6. The second course which makes use of the cinema's peculiar features may branch out in several directions. It will certainly abandon the attempt to convey the whole of an actor's personality; but it may still prefer to use the trained actor for his greater adaptability to artificial conditions; or, alternatively, it may seek natural types and broadly delineate the character of movements instead of deeply penetrating the character of men. It is this main category of the film, however divided, which is the subject of the next two chapters.

Chapter V

Technique of the Film:
1. Analysis

'I am always willing to run some hazard of being tedious in order to be sure that I am perspicuous; and after taking the utmost pains that I can to be perspicuous, some obscurity may still appear to remain upon a subject in its own nature extremely abstracted.'

ADAM SMITH: *The Wealth of Nations*

1. The whole visible world is at the command of the film director.[1] There is no object so large or so small that he cannot compass it with his camera; he may withdraw it until the vastest objects come within its field, or advance it until, with the aid of the microscope, he has sufficiently enlarged the most minute. He need not restrict the sections of the world to their natural places; but may reduplicate them on his strip of film, or juxtapose them even though in nature they were far apart. His records of things as they are, or of multiple movements and composite shots, may be projected on the whole screen, or reduced until the significant part occupies only one-thousandth of its area. In these circumstances, the director is at present compelled to fill the rest of the screen with other mat-

[1]From here to p. 193 it will be assumed, unless otherwise stated, that direction and scenario are undertaken by a single person. The consequences of a separation of function are examined on pp. 193-196, where it is shown that the simplifying assumption introduces errors which are determinate within the limits of accuracy set by the previous discussion.

erial; but the *Magnascope* would increase its margin as the size of the shot was reduced, so that screen and shot expanded and contracted together. However the director may select his natural objects, he can photograph them from an infinite number of camera angles and positions; he can hold them on the screen for as little as a twenty-fourth of a second, or as long as he may wish; if they move, he can greatly accelerate or retard their rate of movement. Plants can be made to spring up from seed to maturity in a few seconds, and racing aeroplanes be so held back that they are many minutes in traversing the screen. The cinema is Behaviourist. The thoughts and emotions to which that psychology denies any real existence are also outside the range of the camera. Only as they are manifested in outward action can they be photographed. Actors must therefore take their place as objects in the physical world, and with these be submitted to the processes just described.

In the same manner, the whole world of sound is at the command of the director: music, speech and song; the noises of animals, the sound of natural forces, wind and rain, waterfalls and seas; of machinery, and the din of the present world; of the countless moving things which, on the stillest night, can be distinguished and marked down. Moreover, the worlds of sight and sound need not be equated realistically. The film allows the freest correlation be-

115

tween visual and auditory records: speech can be continued after the disappearance of the speaker; and, in the manner of opera, music may interpret, by a complex of *leitmotifs*, the broad characteristics of what is shown on the screen. Even when synchronism is rigidly adhered to, it is possible to make a selection of sounds by change of emphasis, fortifying the important and fading the irrelevant to the threshold of audibility.

Such a wealth of material is not at the disposal of any other art, and it constitutes the greatest danger to the status of the film. Hitherto the demands for complete realism on the part of an uneducated public have kept this danger in check; for it will be noticed that, though many of the cinema's powers have an increasingly realistic effect, others, such as those of distortion and non-parallelism, tend in the opposite direction.

But when the film has ultimately become a mere substitute for sense-experience,[1] there is bound to be a revulsion towards a fuller exploitation of its possibilities. One extreme contains the seeds of the other, and the cinema may well degenerate into an example of the incoherent compendia of the arts which flourished after the war. There are two remedies. First, the public can be trained to appre-

[1] See the description of 'The Feelies' in Mr. Huxley's *Brave New World.*

116

ciate that the differences between nature seen and nature filmed constitute the chief value of the cinema and are the source of much of the enjoyment it can provide. Secondly, there is the grasp on the form and functions of the cinema which, if once firmly attained, would deter directors from the useless branches of their art, while leaving them the utmost freedom to express themselves fully in its proper paths.

The film is a dynamic combination of comparatively static units. The units are in their simplest terms still photographs, differing in various determinate respects from the momentary *states* which they record; at the first remove they are representations of *events* and *processes* modified by the differences just mentioned; at the second remove they are additionally modified by differences not inherent in the reproduction of solid objects in a flat plane, but purposely introduced to provide special effects. It is this classification of single shots, and afterwards of their accompanying sounds, which is amplified and subdivided in the present chapter; the dynamic combinations to which film construction gives rise are treated in the next.

2. The film director is continually analysing his material into sections which, in a great variety of ways, can be altered to suit his purpose. At the same time he is synthesizing these sections into larger

units which represent his attitude towards the world, and reveal the design he finds displayed in it. The analysis is an analysis of structure; of the filmic components which the director discerns in the arrangements of the natural world. The synthesis, on the other hand, is a synthesis of effect; of the building up of a mental structure from the emotional and intellectual units it contains. The synthesis determines the analysis, and the analysis the synthesis. To the director, as the shape of a film is formed in his mind, the two processes are inextricably one. Nevertheless, for the purpose of description they may be divided, with much gain in clearness and little danger of false abstraction if their real unity be kept in mind.

3. In this division of the subject, the cut takes a different place from its substitutes. For the former, being timeless, has no independent existence; while the latter are entities having a finite duration. Thus the importance of the cut lies, not in itself, but in the effect which is generated by the juxtaposition of the shots it divides; it is therefore considered in the next chapter. The wipe, the fade and the dissolve, however, are of the same kind as the single shot and take their place in front of it in this chapter. It is necessary only to bear in mind that they produce a softening effect, an indeterminate space between successive shots, which interferes with the establishment

of a recognizable rhythm of shot-lengths, and precludes the occurrence of rhythmical montage.[1] This is a constant defect which will reduce their balance of innate advantage or convert it into a deficit.

The combination of the fade-out with the fade-in is the simplest method of marking the termination of an incident or of a defined period of time. It is therefore not likely to be applied more than eight or ten times in an hour, and there will generally be little doubt of the rightness or wrongness of its use in a particular situation. The dissolve is far more debatable; partly because it is of more frequent occurrence, and partly because more variable elements are involved in its use. Thus the preceding and succeeding shots may be superimposed for any length of time and with any degree of relative intensity; the rates of growth and decay may vary widely, as also may the amount of contrast or similarity between the contents of the shots concerned. Where the complexity of the question is so great, and the application to instances so individual, it is only possible to give general guidance, which may be modified by numerous exceptions.

The dissolve, by slurring over the bridge from shot to shot, markedly reduces any cutting-tone which might otherwise be produced. If, therefore, it is necessary to treat a subject with solemnity, and at

[1]For definition, see p. 51 above.

the same time divide it into short shots (which, as we shall argue below, pp. 219-220, is improbable), the dissolve will provide a solution. If, again, it is necessary to track up several miles to an object (say, a house among the hills) which was just discernible in the first shot, a series of dissolving shots taken from fixed points along the line joining the first to the last shot of the series will admirably produce the required effect. (There appears to be no perfect example of this procedure; but see *The Sea-Shell and the Clergyman* and the opening sequence of *Storm Over Asia.*) Thirdly, if it is required to emphasize the passage of time, it is possible to dissolve through similar objects in scenes which otherwise contrast. (In *A Nous la Liberté*, the progress of the successful ex-convict from a small gramophone shop upwards to the management of a vast gramophone factory was displayed by dissolving from one turntable to another, each revolving in a more resplendent machine than its predecessor, and exhibited in a more magnificent show-room.)

These are legitimate uses, and the list of them is not exhaustive; but they may serve to show that the miscellaneous application of dissolves in the commercial cinema is dictated only by the slovenly attitude of mind 'We've had twenty cuts running now. How about a dissolve or two for a change?' This is likely to be the reason for the average dissolve; it is almost certain to be the sole excuse for a wipe. At least twelve types of wipe may be easily distinguished; and it would require prolonged thought and experiment to justify even one or two of these, and in only very occasional circumstances. We return to this in a moment. But there is a general objection to the wipe. The cut is in the strictest sense imperceptible, and is only a logical abstraction; the wipe, on the other hand, by hypothesis, occupies a perceptible period of time. In this it resembles the dissolve, but, unlike the dissolve, it draws attention to the surface on which it appears; it makes the screen resemble the upper side of a calendar, a solid object from which pictures may be successively torn, the process of tearing being visible. By thus drawing attention to the reality of the screen, the wipe tends in part to distract the mind from the projected images, and in part to 'materialize' them; so that not only is the contrast of transference rendered less acute, but the reality of the shots in themselves is impaired. The spectator is normally able to enter into the thoughts and feelings of persons represented in screen images, which become living, even though ephemeral, entities; once let them dwindle to a series of pictures piled up into calendar form, and they will appear as thin and insubstantial as the books of displaced drawings which, flicked rapidly over, give children the illusion of life.

This is not an objection which is likely to carry much weight with filmgoers of average sensibility; but the advantages which it has to outweigh are also slight. Right and left wipes are the only types which need consideration; and the occasions on which they excel the plain cut are very infrequent. Thus, it may be required to show a person walking through a succession of streets, the shots to be taken from fixed camera positions. In this case, cutting may give the impression that a different person is being seen in each shot, particularly if dusk renders the person's features indistinguishable, and if several other wanderers are known to be in the neighbourhood. In these circumstances it may be better to proceed as follows. The character crosses the screen slowly, say from left to right. When he has covered three-quarters of the distance, a left wipe travels towards him at four times his own speed, and thus reaches him exactly as he passes out of the shot. Meanwhile, the second shot which is steadily appearing (and which shows a visibly different street) contains a man walking at the same speed as the other and in the same direction. The two men will be immediately apprehended as identical, and a feeling of confusion would be aroused if their appearances were dissimilar. (See instances in *The Lodger* (sound version), and a basically similar, though superficially different, example in *Rien que les Heures* (Cavalcanti, 1926), where the gradual decline of food towards the rubbish-bin is quickly and neatly traced by means of wipes.) It remains to add that though, as in the case of the dissolve, legitimate uses of the wipe are rare, examples on the screen abound, and show a complete failure to grasp the needs of particular situations. For *Le Chapeau de Paille d'Italie* and *The Battleship Potemkin* the cut proved sufficient; less harm would be done if those directors were confined to it who are incapable of discovering the proper uses of its alternatives.

In connection with these alternatives, a specimen may be given of the extraordinary fallacies which confused thinking in cinema discussion provokes. Mr. Leonard Hacker writes in *film art*:[1] 'The Dissolve[2] is a physio-chemical device where the Cut is but physical. It is only recently that the laws of chemistry and those of physics have been united in a single science with the realization that all life is both physical and chemical in constant interaction. The Dissolve naturally manifests this unity and thus becomes the true basis of the cinema with the cut and other devices as incidental.' It must be supposed on this argument that the benighted Greeks, who were ignorant not only of biochemistry but of inorganic chemistry, should have abandoned art,

[1]Spring 1934, p. 27.
[2]Dissolves are occasionally produced by a chemical process.

since their knowledge of its true foundation, and hence their scale of values, were miserably tenuous. In modern times, no doubt, the arts in which physics and chemistry combine are greater than those in which they subsist alone. Thus poker-work is to be preferred to sculpture, push-pin ranks at last with poetry, and a book written originally in ink is better than the same book done in pencil. In the superficial manner of the passage quoted, a noteworthy scale of values results, most satisfying to the modern mind. Looked at more closely, however, this apparently solid structure of thought begins to break up. The basis of the film is in any case chemical, for it depends on changes in the constitution of light-sensitive silver compounds. The ink which was the biochemical product of small insects is really no more chemical than the lead out of which pencils are made. Degrees of 'chemicality' cannot be established, since it is impossible to count the number of backward stages, or estimate the importance to be assigned to each. A contention such as this can nowhere be attacked with certainty, since it is founded on faith and argued by evasion.

4. The literary elements of the film must also be considered in advance of the main subject of this chapter, the discussion of the differentiating factors. The credit titles, which are as a rule impatiently dismissed, provide much valuable information to the

spectator. Though it is improbable that the names of assistant story-writers will awake any answering chord in his mind, the names of those responsible for the direction, scenario and camera are usefully committed to memory. It is difficult to determine the conjunction of sight and sound which best conveys these preliminary titles to the audience. The most elaborate method is to make a full sequence of them, beginning and ending perhaps with the trademark of the producing company; the only perfect example of this procedure occurs in the Ufa film *The Blue Angel*. Others prefer to accompany their titles by a 'signature tune' (*e.g.* London Film Productions, which uses the chimes of Big Ben to dispel the cosmopolitan atmosphere of its production staff). Others again attempt to anticipate the mood of the film by an appropriate musical score; this is probably the best method. But, whichever device is chosen, the first necessity is to reduce the number and complexity of credit titles. Only three names are at all likely to be remembered by the public, and these would make a greater impression if they stood in greater isolation. The other names are of importance only to the trade, which is already informed of them through its own periodicals.

The cast is in a special position. There are three main ways of displaying its names: first, and most popular to-day, is to string the list diagonally across the screen, making no reference to parts; this is the worst method, for it neither enlightens ignorance nor supplements knowledge. Second, the players may be set out opposite their parts, as in a theatrical programme; this is effective as far as the important characters are concerned. Thirdly, a method lately revived, preliminary shots of the principal characters are shown, their names being strip-titled on the screen; though the actors are in this way most likely to be remembered, the impression they make is often marred by the futile gestures and impotent mouthings which are allowed to appear; stills should of course be substituted for excerpts from the film.

What is really needed is, however, a complete revision of this part of the film. The practice of discontinuous performance, which is extremely desirable on other grounds, would make possible the use of printed programmes, so that the film might open with its name and the name of its director alone. Little need be said of the structural aspects of the other types of title. They should be brief, cogent, idiomatic, plainly printed on a plain background. Any attempt to create atmosphere by adornments and archaic lettering is almost certain to fail. The use of titling involves many other problems, belonging to the sphere of effect, and these are treated in the next chapter.

126

5. Cuts interrupt the uniform flow of life in its transference to the screen, causing a discontinuity, whose effect is considered in the next chapter, and leaving continuous portions of the film, the shots which register, with greater or less divergence from the original, the states and processes of nature. These divergences, like the equally fundamental divergence of discontinuity, are the condition of the film's status as an art. Art is everywhere present where the natural course of events is arrested and modified by the intelligent action of man. There is art in the building of a bridge, though none in the calculation of the stresses it will bear; in the making of a table, but not in its use when it has become a completed object.

But the name Art is usually, and rightly, reserved for an extension of this simple concept. There are moments of delight in natural happenings, and occasionally in visions, which the artist feels impelled to arrest and transfigure into a permanent material form. What he has seen is not to be measured with rulers or weighed in scales; it is conditioned by his personality, and reflects every aspect of the complex of his faculties and environment. It is therefore not to be expected that a process which depends on accurate reproduction, or even on distortion to a given formula, can be more than technical; it can never attain to art. And as the cinema is in future deprived of one after another of its means of modification of nature, artists, becoming ever more cramped, will forsake it for other arts. This is not to say that that work is greatest which takes greatest liberties with its subject; the artist must have all his powers under his control, but they must be manifold and free if he is to infuse his purpose and character into the beings of nature, so to change them that their life becomes more living, their meaning more significant, their value more sure and true.

6. The differences between nature seen and nature filmed are here called differentiating factors,[1] or 'factors' for short, where there is no danger of ambiguity.[2] These may be divided into optical and non-optical factors. The former class is again divisible into natural factors, inseparable from the representation of natural objects, through the medium of a camera, on the flat surface of a screen; and filmic factors, or differences which may be added to the others as the director desires. The latter class, the non-optical factors (remembering that we have excluded the province of sound), consists of appeals to the senses of smell, taste and touch, which are not at present within the competence of the cinema. They

[1] In preference to Herr Arnheim's synonymous 'formative media', a term which appears less expressive and might therefore be more easily forgotten.

[2] See Chart at the end of the book.

are demanded only by those who believe art to be an inundation of the whole being, deadening the intelligence so that the appetites of the body can be more effectively stimulated and satisfied. This view is so uncommonly held, and is so distasteful, that no arguments are necessary to answer it; it has been finally exposed by Aldous Huxley in his account of 'The Feelies' in *Brave New World*.

But there is another part of the coenaesthesis[1] whose absence from the film is less easily dismissed. Bodily movements, especially those which demand exertion, are accompanied by muscular sensations which give them their peculiar quality. To this cause is due the commonplace observation that photographs of hills give an impression of steepness inferior to that which was felt by the photographer. A man standing upon the slope of a hill is aware of a strain and balance which contribute more to his feeling of steepness than do his purely visual impressions. Where, then, steepness is to be emphasized on the film, the normal record must be supplemented by other material. An excellent example of a method of meeting this difficulty, and at the same time calling forth that imaginative power which creates the work of art, was to be found in *The Blue Light*. A villager was to be seen forcing his way up the steep

[1]The general sense of existence arising from the sum of bodily impressions.

side of Monte Cristallo, struggling over rocky surfaces and pressing on with his utmost energies to reach the mysterious light which shone from the summit. The sound factor, here musical, conveyed a sense of labour and strain from the strings, while, in the visual film, there were shots of the man's fingers clawing and digging into the crevices of the rock.

Another example, of a different type, may be imagined. The scraping of a knife on a plate produces an unpleasant grating sensation, whose intensity seems out of all proportion to the intensity of the stimulus. But a closely similar sensation often arises when the teeth are being scraped and drilled. If, then, the discomfiture of the dental patient were to be displayed, the visible signs, such as the slight contraction of facial muscles, should be paralleled in the sound factor, not by the soothing hum of the dentist's drill, but by the sound of a knife scraping on a plate.[1] (This is an instance of the evocative branch of the selective use of sound.)

In ways such as these the absence of the other senses is to be compensated by audible and optical means. Close-up photography of silk, or wrinkled skin, or dough being squeezed and moulded, will, under proper conditions of lighting, produce a tact-

[1] It is this type of small but interesting experiment which could usefully be undertaken by amateurs possessing sound-recording equipment.

ual sensation which strongly reinforces the visual. The sense of smell is difficult of translation. It is one of the strongest means of recapturing lost memories, or of strengthening those which have grown dim; but as the smell is usually linked with the remembered event by a chance association, it will awake no answer in the spectator. There is therefore little urgency to solve this problem; but in a few cases, such as the hay-field in summer, the film might be so vividly presented that, the scent of hay with all its memories being brought to mind, this effect would react upon the other and heighten the impression of the whole.

Taste, again, is comparable with touch in the manner in which it may be evoked. Touch responds to the corrugations which compose the texture of a surface, by minute sensations usually conveyed from the tips of the fingers. Tactual contact brings the eyes close enough to observe the quality of what is touched; and often the enjoyment of texture, as for instance the irregularly broken segments of the bark of trees, is not completed until the fingers have been run over the surface. Finally, as we have seen, when the tactual stimuli have been removed, they persist through their visual counterparts. So also with taste; for hunger, unless extreme, heightens the visual impressions of what is eaten.

7. The natural factors are resolved into the static

and dynamic,[1] those which operate on still photographs, and those additionally which operate when the camera or its subject, or both, are in motion. The primary division in the first class concerns the camera at rest. The camera is the eye of the director. However skilfully he chooses his cast, cuts his film or weaves his sound into it, there will remain an element of the random or disordered if he has not determined each camera angle and position by his interpretation of the subject chosen. This has led to the statement by Herr Arnheim: 'Since it is incumbent upon the film director to decide upon an angle of approach, he has the power of selecting what objects he will allow to appear in the picture; to conceal what he does not wish to show, or does not wish to show at once; . . . to bring into prominence and give the central position to whatever he considers to be important and which very possibly would not of itself show its importance in the scene . . . without (*sc.* his) being obliged to interfere with the objects themselves or to alter them in any way.'[2] This passage gives a good impression of the freedom with which the director accords his camera to the elements of the subject which create the mood of his recorded scene.

A somewhat different view is expressed by Mr.

[1]See Chart at the end of the book.
[2]*Op. cit.* pp. 59-60.

Rotha: 'The choice of an angle cannot be a disputed point or even a matter of opinion. Provided the mood of an image and its connection with the sequence is clearly indicated by the scenario-plan, there is only *one* position in which the camera can be placed in order to render that shot most expressive of the mood required.'[1]

This assertion, though approximately true, is not very illuminating until an important tacit assumption has been made plain. The feelings of one person are in the strictest sense incommensurable, both in quality and intensity, with the feelings of another person; this is a truth upon which philosophy, psychology, and even common sense, are agreed. If, then, the scenarist and the director (who is assumed to decide the camera position) are not identical persons, the following process is involved in the determination of the *one* position already mentioned. The director makes the utmost endeavour to appreciate the mood which the scenarist desires; but, as his feelings are strictly incomparable with the scenarist's, there must remain a field of error, large or small as the degree of co-operation is slight or intense. In order to narrow down this field, the director must arrange the numerous components of his subject in every way which falls within his limits of error, and shoot them from every different angle and position.

[1] *The Film Till Now*, p. 275.

There are so many independent variables in question that thousands of different strips would have to be exposed if the one shot which aroused in the scenarist the exact mood which he had envisaged previously were to be discovered. In practice, of course, this lengthy process is much abbreviated, so that there results only a very imperfect correspondence between what the scenarist has required and what the director has given him.

When the conditions are narrowed by assuming that the director and scenarist are one party, an error in Mr. Rotha's statement becomes visible, though concealed by complications before. It is only a person of infinite, and so of superhuman, sensibility who could appreciate the difference in mood caused by an infinitely small displacement of the camera. Hence, for all actual human beings, there will be a finite volume in which the camera may move, and throughout which they will be indifferent as to its final position. Directors of small ability will be satisfied if the camera is very approximately placed; but more competent men (*pace* Mr. Rotha) will quarrel with their decision if they are upon the boundaries of error. Hence the better director (here defined by the smallness of his field of indifference) may always be in a position to dispute the decisions of the worse; but not, it would seem, *vice versa*. On reflection, however, it appears that even this opportunity of agreement is not assured. The incompetent director may have misconceived the necessities of a scene, though clearly expressed in the scenario; and this is frequently apparent on the screen. Directors of equal standing, moreover, may well argue the relative value of two camera positions to bring out a mood on which both (subject to the limitations mentioned above) are agreed. One, for instance, may discover an object of symbolic importance in the scene before him, and desire to emphasize it; the other, of a more realistic turn of mind, will obscure it from view. Thus the foregoing argument, far from being fanciful or academic, demonstrates the fact that disputes as to camera position may legitimately arise between directors of similar temperament but different ability, and still more radical disputes when both temperament and ability are different. Though, in fact, there is one position which will convey a given mood more expressively than any other, it is not possible for any human being either to determine it precisely, or to place it above dispute, unless both he and his critics are men precisely similar in every material respect; and this is a condition which under no circumstances can be fulfilled.

If this is the case, then *a fortiori* a statement of Mr. Hunter's must be false. 'The use of camera angles, as far as it has progressed at present, approximates the cinema far nearer to science than art. A good film tends to be more constructive than creative. Theoretically there is only one angle from which to photograph each scene; the choice of this angle cannot be a disputed point or even a matter of opinion. This surely is a kind of knowledge which can be acquired by experience, and approaches far nearer to science than art.'[1] If there is no practical possibility of even subjective agreement, an objective standard or a mathematical formula is bound to fail. A result of the increasingly scientific habits of thought to-day has been a failure to realize the limitations of scientific method. In fact, there is no reason to suppose that the choice of a camera angle is not perfectly free, just as the choice of a word or phrase of music is free. Two writers, asked to convey the same mood, will employ widely different means; some readers will prefer one, some the other; and, if the writers are men of ability, it may be impossible to establish an agreed order of precedence between them. Let us suppose, however, that the experimental psychologist discovered some method (say, for simplicity, the change of electrical resistance in the body) of 'measuring' emotion; that is to say, a larger fall of resistance was found experimentally to coincide with an intenser feeling of emotion on the ap-

[1]*Scrutiny of Cinema*, p. 21, at the conclusion of a chapter entitled *Towards a Criticism of the Cinema*.

plication of emotive stimuli; and *vice versa*. Mr. Hunter's assertion that camera angles can be scientifically determined would be realized if the bridge circuit used to measure resistance were attached to the director as he moved hither and thither over his set, looking at it from every possible angle. At the point where the galvanometer indicated the largest fall of resistance the camera would be set up. This method has that appearance of scientific value which is demanded for an art making a calculated appeal to the spectator, and built up, like advertisement, on an elaborate estimate of 'what the public wants'. But its real value is quite specious and fanciful. For a reason already given,[1] a method such as this can only be applied to the group of people from the 'measurement' of whose emotions the method has itself been established. If the director is one of this group the galvanometer will only show what was already known to him, and with much greater precision and certainty, by introspection. If he is not a member of the group, the method is wholly fallacious and uncertain.

It will now be abundantly clear that no deterministic method of fixing the camera can be sound. There is every possibility of disputing about tastes, if only because there is no means of deciding them. Freedom of choice, however, denotes freedom to record every shade of temperament and character.

[1]See p. 133, ll. 10-14, above.

The camera at rest has innumerable powers. Even if the arrangement of objects set before it is fixed, it can be placed as a rule so as to conceal what is large, or reveal what is so small that the eye unaided would have overlooked it. The close-up, which film writers have incessantly hailed as a signal enlargement of the powers of the cinema, is frequently attacked by those whose profession is the stage. It is, say the latter, a crude device by which the actors evade their duty of drawing attention to important small objects by subtle movements and pauses. This criticism cannot be ignored, particularly when it refers to films which draw their inspiration from the theatre. The object of the average director is to convey his meaning to the spectator so plainly that the dullest wit cannot fail to be aware of it. The close-up is a godsend: a finger pointed here and there to mark the important details of a scene. But this is a clumsy scheme of presentation. The finest and deepest impressions are the reflections which glance unspoken from character to character, and the implications which arise only in the spectator's mind, and are blunted and damaged by materialization.[1]

8. This is a warning; it must not be elevated into a maxim. Mr. Hunter remarks: 'The close-up, too, is accepted without any consideration of the limitations it may imply. It is true that if the close-up is con-

[1] Cf. *The Cherry Orchard* as a film subject.

demned on principle, so too must be the long shot and the medium shot, or any other form of selection. But if one sees a close-up of a woman's eyes when she is crying there seems to be no logical reason why one may not reasonably expect a radiograph of her mind, natural colours, etc., etc., *ad infinitum*.'[1] But what is the 'principle' or 'logical reason' to which Mr. Hunter appeals? Even if it could be clearly stated, of what value would it be when, as Mr. Hunter implies, it would condemn painting, photography and film alike, depending as they do on selection, and on departure from perfect naturalism? And of what value is this argument, based on an absurd assumption, except to ridicule an opinion which no one has ever held?

In reality, the use of the close-up extends from obviousness to obscurity. On the one hand, the director may select an object for detailed inspection, and hold it as long on the screen as he would have held the whole scene of which the object was a minute part; a common occurrence when the mind of the stage is applied to the methods of the film. And, on the other hand, the close-up may so isolate its subjects from their surroundings that they float disembodied and unrelated to one another; this tends to confusion. But there is a middle way, in which the close-up forces the spectator into intimate

[1] *Op. cit.* pp. 20-21.

contact with the screen images, which are cut together sufficiently rapidly to present new material to the mind as fast as it can grasp it, and to realize the benefits of rhythmical montage. This method has long been known to the Russian directors, who have made of it an increasingly powerful weapon. The crowd is no longer, as in British and American films, an undifferentiated mass. If it waits on the words of a speaker, the camera, flashing from one part of it to another, discovers one man expectant, another already assured, a third confident of disappointment; the film, running in perfect silence, catches the tension of all. The opening phrases are spoken; confirmation, reluctant approval or contempt is marked on the listeners' faces as shot is built up on to shot, the cuts contributing their effect by their heightened speed. A struggle breaks out; the whirl of bodies, blurred by the closely swinging camera, is matched to the thud of blows and the impotent shouting of the speaker.[1]

The mass is split up and its elements are combined; the individual is revealed in many aspects to be synthesized into a whole which is only then comprehensible. The cinema, so far as it is visual, is debarred access to all thoughts and emotions; and though, by montage, it can transcend material particulars, it can do so only when they are sufficiently

[1]Part of a sequence in *Deserter*.

explicit and detailed. The close-up, as well in time as in space, arrests the outward signs of feeling; a touch of slow motion reveals the beauty hidden in a smile which was gone too quickly for the eye; and a glance at a restless foot or a contracted brow indicates what the film cannot directly express. Banality often lies dangerously near; but genius can as well avoid it in the cinema as it can redeem the commonplace plates and oranges which are among the subjects of still life.

9. We may turn now to the delimitation of the screen. The visual field presented by the eyes is roughly circular in shape, being most clearly defined at the centre, and fading away to the fringes of indirect vision. But though the field is in fact thus circumscribed, it can so readily be extended by movements of the head as to become for most purposes unrestricted. The screen, on the other hand, is sharply bounded by its margins, which the spectator cannot by any effort expand or transfer. The process of selection is consequently of extreme importance; for an audience which is bound to observe the section of space presented to it will be unusually critical of the compositions it contains. This consideration applies much less forcibly to the stage, where the major arrangements of material are maintained intact for upwards of half an hour. Within this fixed framework, the patterns of grouping and colour come and go; and the spectator is free to delimit them by the

141

mechanism of attention in the manner in which he appreciates them best. In the cinema, however, this process is largely transferred to the director, who advances and retreats his camera until the patterns he has chosen are exactly embraced within its view. If, then, the spectator feels that he is looking through a small rectangular hole on to a stage, of which he would be glad to see more, the director has altogether failed in his task; but if each shot carries with it inevitability and compelling authority, it will be accepted and absorbed with critical appreciation. This was strongly apparent in the miscellaneous collection of shots from Eisenstein's Mexican epic, where fresh shapes were continually revealed in the curves of the peons' hats, and the rising and drooping leaves of aloes.

In view of this importance of composition, it is essential that the best shape of screen be found and adhered to. The artist is free within the infinite horizontal latitude of the bas-relief or the Japanese landscape woodcut, or the considerable vertical latitude of the tallest Gothic window. Even in the sphere of Western painting, much diversity of ratio of height to length is permissible, varying commonly between about $1 \cdot 6 : 1$ and $1 : 1 \cdot 6$. In the cinema, however, the proportions of each composition must remain the same, and their size must be the same during a given projection. In 1930 the shape of the screen was the subject of discussion in Hollywood, when the universal adoption of the wide film was being debated. It was ultimately rejected on economic grounds, when it was found that the increased audiences to be attracted by the exceptional 'grandeur' of the new film would not pay for the extensive alterations to cinemas necessitated by the wider screen. This final but uninteresting objection was not, however, raised until Eisenstein had read a paper on the subject, in which a number of aesthetic and psychological issues were very acutely examined. Only the barest summary of the arguments can be given here, and the reader is referred for fuller details to *Close-Up*, March and June 1931. Eisenstein draws attention to the fact that, though at present vertical compositions are impossible, they have played an important part in the development of man. The contemptible has always been represented by the low and crawling; indeed the very words 'base' and 'low', though they now have a separate metaphorical meaning, are indicative of the horizontal. Contrasted with this, man acquired a new footing when he became *homo erectus*; his progress was always 'higher'; he looked up into the heavens to God, and manifested his aspiration in Gothic arches, spires and windows. In the new industrial age he typified the spirit of materialism in factory chimneys, skyscrapers and pylons.

But though the vertical is dominant, the lure of

the horizontal is not dead. Horizons, plains and the boundless stretches of the sea still breed nostalgia, bringing memories of lands untouched by the urgency and speed of modern life. To resolve this conflict, Eisenstein advocates the *square* screen, which would treat impartially compositions which are internally either vertical or horizontal. He demolishes convincingly the arguments in favour of the existing proportions; that statistical investigation of the shape of large numbers of paintings shows the average ratio of base to altitude to be 1·5 : 1; that the 'golden square' rectangle (1·667 : 1) has predominated in the arts for centuries because of its inherent dynamism; that the normal visual field tends to be horizontal because it is easier to 'pan' the eyes than to 'tilt' them. These arguments are refuted by contending that (1) averages have no value for such a purpose when the dispersal about the mean is so wide; (2) the dynamism inherent in the cinema (*e.g.* rhythmical montage) needs no assistance from a peculiar proportion in the single shot; (3) the eye is assisted to 'tilt' by movements of the head, so that it turns as easily on one axis as on the other.

The square screen would thus seem to be successfully vindicated; but at a vital point in the argument Eisenstein becomes contradictory and obscure. He says: 'The only and unique form (*i.e.* the square) equally fit by alternate suppression of right and left, or of up and down, to embrace all the multitude of expressive rectangles of the world. Or used as a whole to engrave itself by its "cosmic" imperturbability of its *squareness* in the psychology of the audience. . . .

'Note here 1: This means that dynamism of changeable proportion of the projected picture is accomplished by masking a part of the shape of the film-square—the frame.

'And note here 2: This has nothing to do with the suggestion that the proportions 1 : 2 (3 : 6) give a "vertical possibility" in masking the right and the left to such an extent that the remaining area has the form of an upright standing strip. The *vertical spirit* can never thus be attained; 1st: because the occupied space comparative to the horizontal masked space will never be interpreted as something *axially opposed* to it, but always *as a part* of the latter, and 2nd: for, *never surpassing the height* that is bound to the horizontal dominant, it will never impress as an opposite space axis—the one of uprightness.'[1] (Italics throughout in the original.)

10. Eisenstein here appears at first to be commending and then combating the proposal (made at another time) for an expanding screen. The truth (perhaps expressed under 'Note here 2' above) seems to be as follows. A constantly shifting set of margins

[1]*Op. cit.* pp. 7-8.

would not appear basically to alter the compositions which they framed; they would merely introduce a black, masking element which would seem part of the shot itself. They would thus be analogous to the picture frame of which the spectator is definitely and consciously aware, instead of noticing it merely as a boundary to the picture. If this be true, no good purpose will be served by seeking to aid a vertical composition by a vertical screen, and then immediately a horizontal by a horizontal; the original square would have proved equally effective, while allowing more to be included in the shot.

On the other hand, it is possible that a screen which only very occasionally expanded might produce some heightening of dramatic effect. Even here, however, it is the relative size of the two shots which is important, and this can nearly always be secured far more readily by a close-up. Not unless it is essential that the same content be shown at a greater size (or of course a greater content at the same size) can the expanding screen be justified. We conclude, therefore, that a square screen would be a valuable acquisition for the cinema, but that the Magnascope can be easily dispensed with as having little more than a novelty appeal.

11. We turn next to the problems of colour and lighting. It is often objected to aesthetic theory that, so long as it is content to describe, it does nothing

more than state in complicated abstract terms what the reader already knew; but that when it attempts to predict, its findings are almost always falsified by subsequent events. We have tried to show in Chapter I that the first part of this assertion gives a very inaccurate account of the uses of descriptive aesthetics; but against the second charge little answer can be made. In physics, predictions are not only possible, but often accurate; the irregularities in the path of Neptune can be used to estimate the mass and the period of revolution of an unknown, in the sense of invisible, planet. But in aesthetics, causes produce effects out of all proportion to their apparent magnitude; so that, although every large factor introduced by a change may have been imagined and allowed for, some small neglected detail will upset the anticipated results.

Colour has not yet been introduced on an extensive scale; the most notable examples of it, the recent Silly Symphonies, having, as we shall show, been produced under circumstances quite different from the natural. The conclusions reached here must therefore be regarded as extremely tentative; they rest on considerations which should certainly be borne in mind, but which may have to be very differently weighted in the light of future experience. These remarks are to be taken as prefatory also to the next differentiating factor, flatness.

It seems at first sight that colour and solidity, unlike sound, introduce differences only of degree. Colour is a multiplication of the single colour-scale black-white; stereoscopy an intensification of a solidity which is already partially apparent in perspective and in motion perpendicular to the plane of the screen. Sound, however, was a radical addition to the silent film, fulfilling a function which had no counterpart before. Such considerations have led Eisenstein, Pudovkin and others to hold that the third of these factors was incomparably more important than the first two. Logically, however, this contention appears to rest on a fallacy; for, examined more closely, the function of sound will be seen to have been undertaken in the silent film by titles and pictorial counterparts, just as a diversity of colour values is now rendered by a single scale. Moreover, as we shall see presently, stereoscopy will be a much more formidable barrier to montage than was the advent of sound.

If a number of painters were set successively to paint a scene from the same place, and under the same conditions of lighting, it is certain that their results would differ widely not only in line, but in colour distribution and value. They would have made use, that is to say, of their power to impose a subjective design on scientifically measurable material objects; and in so far as their subjective approaches were different, their completed paintings would be different. We are in the process of discussing here the differentiating factors which in the cinema correspond to the painter's free use of line and colour; and it is our present contention that the introduction of colour in the film would not be accompanied by any additions, valuable as they would be, to this list of factors.

The painter, whom we assume throughout to be in some degree naturalistic, will be able to designate any given colour in nature by any colour whatever on his canvas. There will be some correspondence on the above assumption between the *shape* of a patch of colour in nature, defined by its spatial relations to other such patches, and another patch of colour on the canvas, similarly defined; but there will be no necessary correspondence between the *colours* of these patches. (Or, of course, naturalism might be defined in terms of fixed colour, and variable spatial relations.) In the cinema, however, it appears that, at a first approximation, the colour correspondence is fixed. The emulsion, which was arranged by its maker to produce a particular colour when affected by light of a particular frequency, cannot be altered by the director. In the matter of colour, therefore, the painter has a wider and more powerful choice than the photographer, as he has in turn (in this respect) over the worker in black and white alone.

The colour photograph or film has no greater independence than the black-to-white film, and its superiority must be justified on other grounds.

We can now take a step nearer to reality. We have hitherto assumed that an object of a given colour could only be reproduced in monochrome with a single distribution along the colour-scale. This is no more than a first approximation. Lighting can be used to throw parts of an object into shadow, and thus raise the others into bright relief. Filters can correct deficiencies in the colour rendering of emulsions, or they can overcorrect in order to provide some desired colour alteration (*e.g.* the black skies often to be seen in Russian films). Detail can be made evident, or attention concentrated on some important part of a scene; even apparent distortion in space can be created by the use of light. These powers will no doubt be transferable to the colour film, and thus do not weigh either for or against it. Two objections, however, may be suggested, which will carry the more weight the more important the application of colour is likely to prove. And even if the splendours of painting are set aside on the ground that they afford a far freer choice of colour than the film, the enjoyment of natural scenery is so greatly intensified by colour that it could not but make a great difference even in a fixed application to the cinema.

First, by introducing another complicating element into the cinema, without at the same time increasing its differentiating factors, there would be a distinct tendency towards greater naturalism. This, on the criteria already mentioned, would be retrogressive. Second, and arising out of the first objection, colour as a fixed additional factor would slow down the construction of the film. The complexities of a multiple colour-scale cannot be apprehended nearly so quickly as can monochrome. Hence, in order to allow for a full appreciation of each shot, it will have to be continued for a further length of time, and the exceptionally short shots, which contribute so much to the variation of tempo, and the building of specific effects, upon which most of the excellence of the film depends, must be sacrificed. This argument is by no means conclusive. As composition is simplified, it can be arranged as a rule that patterns of colour are simplified also; all that is contended is that colour will always lag behind monochrome, causing the effect of each shot to reach its maximum more slowly, and consequently deferring the cutting point.[1] This objection could evidently be removed if the director were at liberty to discard colour as soon as his cutting demanded it; but so radical a change would no doubt be very disturbing and would almost certainly outweigh the advantages gained.

[1]See pp. 215-219 below.

12. The synthetic film escapes altogether the first of these disabilities, and suffers less heavily from the second. The director (if the term can be applied to one whose sole resources are paint, paper, cameras and assistants) can choose his colours as freely as can the painter. Disney has already provided many examples of the subjective, non-naturalistic use of colour (e.g. *The Babes in the Wood*, when the witch falls out of the sky into a cauldron of boiling liquid, and undergoes the most entertaining changes of colour in the process of cooling on the ground). Rapid rhythmical montage has not yet been attempted in a synthetic film, but colour would here be less of a hindrance than in a naturalistic film, since it is so easily simplified.

It seems on the whole, therefore, that colour would increase the beauty of individual shots, though by an amount enormously less than the superiority in this respect of painting over monochromatic photography; but that such an increase of beauty is contrary to the real needs of the cinema, unless it can be controlled in degree, and removed where necessary. This is not at all easily achievable. Colour may well raise the standard of poor films; but the better the film the smaller will be the gain. Synthetic films, on the other hand, are almost certain to gain from the adoption of colour.

13. The next factor is flatness. This is a particu-

larly difficult subject to treat clearly, because it hinges on questions of degree not very widely separated. The film of to-day exhibits a higher degree of solidity than the silent film, but a lower degree than that of binocular vision. Flatness has the advantage of concentrating the attention on to spatial relations in a single plane, and so of divorcing it from the perception of normal life. It is thus possible to impose on natural objects a significance they did not present to the unguided spectator, but which the artist is able to capture and render plain. Thus Pudovkin, in *The End of St. Petersburg*, has a shot depicting the entrance into the city of two starving peasants, looking for work. In the foreground is an apparently vast equestrian statue of a Tsar, and the littleness of the figures passing it is a forcible suggestion of the loneliness and bewilderment of the peasants. Herr Arnheim[1] observes that if the film possessed a greater degree of apparent solidity this effect would never arise. For it would occur to the spectator that it was the obvious distance perpendicular to the screen separating the peasants from the statue which accounted for their apparent disparity in size; and that, if they were placed side by side, the peasants might even be seen to be the larger. This contention is certainly true of the degree of solidity present in human vision; the

[1] *Op. cit.* p. 73.

suggested reflection would occur immediately. Between this and the flatness of the silent film there is an indefinitely graded series; it is only possible to say what effects will characterize this scale in greater or less degree, in proceeding from one extreme to the other; it is scarcely possible to say what objections would attach to any particular point on the scale, owing to the difficulties of specific reference.

The first objection to increased solidity we have seen to be the limitations imposed on composition and contrast; the second and third are in principle identical with the two objections to colour (q.v.). The application of the second (the third here) is of course different; solidity does not impose any fresh complexities upon the spectator's appreciation; indeed, by drawing nearer to life, it simplifies his task. It does, however, progressively reduce the possibilities of montage. The shock of transition which we have found to be the basis of rhythmical montage is not due to any feeling of transference through space; this is seen by its appearance in abstract films of the non-spatial variety. Even if this were not true, the extraordinary intensification of the least important type of montage would overshadow the rest, and so reduce the value of the whole film.

14. The effect of a cut in a stereoscopic film would make the spectator feel that he had been lifted up and hurled through space in an instant. In the

limiting case, in which the film is in this respect an exact equivalent of life, this appears obvious. It is a phenomenon so remote from the actual that its effect could only be very disconcerting. To mitigate this to some extent, however, it must be recalled that transfer through space is in part felt because of the bodily feelings (relative movements of objects, muscular sensations, etc.) which normally accompany it. On the other hand, even if the spectator felt himself taken up and deposited elsewhere with the suddenness and convenience of magic, he would be readier to marvel at his transit than to compare what he saw now with what he saw before. The whole value of the cut lies in its imperceptibility,[1] which renders more striking the contrast between adjacent shots. This effect would no doubt diminish in time, but to an unpredictable extent.

It scarcely seems possible to balance these many conflicting considerations with any nicety. The general conclusion, however, when the earlier and more manageable arguments are taken into account, is that any further increase of solidity would do no good, and might do much harm. Sound and speech have certainly resulted in a heightening of the sense of depth; but despite the gloomy prophecies of Herr

[1] See p. 121 above; but note that this word is used in an opposite sense, p. 81 above, where it refers to a smooth transition from one shot to the next.

155

Arnheim,[1] they have scarcely detracted at all from the beneficent influence of distortion on composition.

15. This concludes our examination of the static branch of the natural differentiating factors, and we proceed therefore to the components of the dynamic branch. These, it will be recalled, operate 'when the camera or its subject, or both, are in motion'. It is evident that movement of the camera past the subject will produce precisely the same effect on the spectator as movement of the subject past the camera; in this the film differs from life, where the bodily sensations associated with the two phenomena are distinct and recognizable. It is this which leads people who visit films now for the first time to remark that the scenery is constantly moving; but of course the orientation to a correct view is very rapid.

16. We shall first discuss the motives which apparently lead in the commercial cinema to-day to the wide employment of tracking and panning (defs. A. *b*. 6 and 7), the two most important camera movements; and will thus be able to clear out of the way some pernicious misunderstandings, and find it easier to appreciate (what the Russian directors have known for nearly ten years) the true and limited uses of the moving camera. Throughout the greater part of the normal film, which may be seen at almost every non-specialized cinema in the country, the

[1]*Op. cit.* pp. 236-239.

camera will be found to be in motion. If a character sitting in one room gets up, walks to the door, passes down a corridor into another room, the camera will very often follow the whole series of actions, as if terrified that he will escape. This is supposed to correspond to the mechanism of attention, the camera merely doing what the spectator would do, or would wish to do, if he were present at the scene. A little reflection will show that this is a gross travesty of the truth. If the eyes are attentively watching a certain event, say a person speaking, and if another event, say a movement of the door handle, seems to the mind to be of superior importance, the eyes and head will indeed be turned, but not in the least in the way represented by the camera. The reader should try the experiment for himself, and carefully compare it with observations of tracking and panning in films. The first process (the human) proceeds approximately as follows. At each end of the eye-travel, the field of vision is clear and definite about the area which is being attended to; the periphery of this area becomes, of course, increasingly indistinct as it recedes. But between the two positions is a space which is neither clear nor blurred. It is not apprehended at all; it is a mere blank.

Compare this with camera-travel: first very slowly, then more quickly, then as fast as possible, to discover whether any approach to the previous effect can be achieved. If the camera moves very slowly, the spectator will be able to mark with perfect clearness the objects traversed on the way, with as much clearness, in fact, as the terminal objects. If the panning or tracking is now speeded, a quite different effect is produced. The film passes through the camera and projector at a finite speed, whereas images succeed one another on the retina at a speed which is for all practical purposes infinite. The difference is best brought out by supposing the camera fixed, and its subject moving. Then, one frame or picture-element will record the subject at a specific place, and the next at a place which differs from the first by an amount not imperceptible, but perceived as a jerk. This of course holds good when the camera moves, while its subject is still, and accounts for the jarred, overlapping appearance of objects when the camera fairly rapidly traverses them. The speed of movement of a fixed object across a single frame in the camera (upon which this phenomenon depends) is naturally governed not only by the velocity of the camera (angular or linear according to whether it pans or tracks), but upon its distance from the object. It is thus possible to pan much faster across a distant object than a near one. This effect of overlapping reduplication in the moving shot has no correspondence with the mechanism of attention, but merely evokes an unpleasant sensation in the eye. When the camera moves very rapidly indeed, the effect is yet again different. Objects appear to merge into one another, and are drawn out into long bands[1]; this may on occasion be highly decorative and fascinating, but it has nothing to do with attention.

We conclude, therefore, that if the moving camera is to be justified at all, it must be justified on other grounds. It is noteworthy that the majority of Russian directors scarcely move their cameras at all. In *The Battleship Potemkin*, only the Odessa steps sequence was so shot, (and here the material itself was moving); in the great length of *October* (two and a half hours) there were hardly a dozen moving shots. The majority of non-Russian directors seem to think that if their story is slow and lifeless, it can be made to move merely by moving the camera; in fact, however, this results in a purposeless irritation, the proper procedure being to cut from each point of vital attention to the next. Thereby, the discontinuity which lies at the bottom of nearly all the powers of the film is given its proper weight. The method of flux, on the other hand, approximates closer and closer to the stage the more it is extended; for there the eye follows characters from point to point with perfect smoothness; they never vanish, to reappear the next moment in a different place. This, however,

[1]Two or three examples of this occurred in *The Constant Nymph* (Basil Dean, 1933).

is what happens and must happen in the cinema (not, of course, in a single, but in adjacent shots) if it is to be based on the principles of montage; on the principles of flux, it will enter into competition with the stage, lose its individuality and suffer all the disabilities which were described in Chapter III. It is therefore in connection with montage that the moving camera must be vindicated; the subject will be continued in the next chapter, when the nature of montage has become clearer.

17. Meanwhile the use of tilting can be disposed of. Most of the remarks made above on panning and tracking can be applied to it, but it has a few peculiar functions which are less closely connected with either montage or attention. If it is desired to show that two groups of people, not in sight of one another, are yet in close proximity, the following method, illustrated from *The Road to Life,* is sometimes applicable. A gang of rowdy boys was discovered about to make an attack on a person not in view, the camera tilting down upon the boys across the pillared wall of a large building. There was then a cut to a similar wall, and a similar tilt took place until an old woman selling apples was found sitting by the pavement. The building was thus used to link unmistakably two sets of persons who might otherwise, until the attack took place, have seemed entirely unconnected

A further and more significant use of tilting has

lately been revealed by Stuart Legg. He wished in *Telephone Workers* to show the rapid growth of modern towns which has led to a sudden extension of communications. Fast motion was obviously inappropriate, and a fast-cut series of shots depicting the town at succeeding stages of growth would have been hackneyed and thus largely ineffective. Instead, he tilted slowly down from a region of clear sky across the tops and so across the façades of the new buildings. Owing to the absence of the muscular feelings which accompany movements of the head, the effect was the opposite of that described, and it seemed that buildings were rising up into the field of view. When this had taken place, there was a quick dissolve to another piece of blue sky, and the cycle was repeated. By this simple and natural process, one of the generalizations which the cinema finds it difficult to accomplish was strikingly effected.

18. All the natural differentiating factors have now been examined, and we pass to the filmic factors, in which the freedom of the cinema is most apparent and must be most carefully controlled. The speed at which the film passes through the camera is in no way confined to the fixed speed of projection; it may be either faster or slower by any desired amount. We shall begin with the most extreme fast motion and traverse the spectrum of speeds to the most extreme slow motion.

19. It is evident that the processes of organic growth are continuous movements of the same nature as those we commonly so designate, but of a much greater slowness. To watch the opening of a flower in the morning demands the utmost patience and attention; to watch the springing up of even a mushroom makes a considerable call on the memory of earlier stages by the time that later stages are reached; to watch the growth of a tree is impossible, save by comparing many trees at different stages of their development. The cinema has altered all this. By taking a film at the rate of, say, one frame an hour (instead of twenty-four a second) an increase of speed of nearly ninety thousand times is obtained, and this can easily be exceeded where necessary. If the process is a continuous one, this not only enables it to be watched as a single whole, instead of having to be partially remembered[1]; it ensures that a complete record is obtained. Thus as a scientific weapon, it is of the utmost value; in this capacity it is treated by Miss Field in *Secrets of Nature,* to which the reader is referred. Here we are concerned only with its artistic applications, which are found even in this study of organisms. The beauty of a flower is half realized when it is seen with the eye; the camera reveals fully another half. The sinuous

[1] In philosophical terms, it is embraced in the specious present, instead of extending into the past.

162

movements of the stalk as it twists dexterously in its search for sunlight, the tossing of the head, and the uncoiling and stretching of the fronds of fern; these are delights which have been imagined by poets, but never before seen by other men.[1]

As the camera is slowed down, other phenomena are lighted up by it. The ascent of the moon into the sky, the clearing of the shadow of night from the face of a mountain,[2] are parallel to the instances we have mentioned. To the scientist they are perfectly prosaic; what previously moved too slowly to follow is now accelerated into visibility. But to the poet they may seem to show that the instant vitality which is marked in the thoughts and actions of men extends also to plants and even stones, which to eyes less encompassed by time than ours would display the same activity as we do.

20. Crossing now the neutral point, where velocities are equal on the screen and in life, we reach the region of slow motion. Here the events which flash past so quickly that they are gone before they are apprehended may be slowed down and examined. Scientifically, the moving parts in machinery can be inspected while they are actually running, and subject to the stresses of normal use. Artistically, the

[1]Cf. *Ferns and Fronds* (Mary Field, 1932) and *Miracle of Flowers*.

[2]*The Blue Light* (Leni Riefenstahl, 1931).

fastest and most agile movements, whether of animals leaping or of men diving, can be appreciated closely, instead of being recollected as a momentary glance. A further increase of slow motion enables masses of earth or metal, as in an explosion, to be seen creeping through the air towards the camera, and then, by a sudden reversion to neutral speed, to hurl themselves and overwhelm it.

21. These are the mainly mechanical uses of camera speed, and further instances will readily occur to the mind. But there is a more subtle application of them, which was described by Pudovkin in the early part of 1932, but has scarcely been used at all. Combining fast with slow, it is hinted at in the last example given above. This is the temporal close-up[1]; together with cutting and camera-angle, it properly reproduces the mechanism of attention. The principle involved is as follows. The camera is already used spatially to guide the attention of the spectator (or to *mis*guide him, in order to call out the powerful force of implication); in either case a process of selection is at work, so that the mind, though it may be baulked in order to incite it higher, is never clogged by irrelevance. Temporally, however, the camera has hitherto been content to be neutral; certainly it has shot whole episodes in slow-motion, but this is no more refined artistically than shooting them wholly

[1]Pudovkin, *op. cit.* pp. 146-154.

in close-up. What is wanted is guidance not only in space but in time; the arresting of movements on which the eye wishes to linger, the accelerating of those which depend on their flashing speed.

A single example, the simplest, from Pudovkin can be given here. 'I tried to shoot and edit the rain in the same way. . . . The slow striking of the first heavy drops against dry dust. They fall, scattering into separate dark globules. The falling of rain on a surface of water: the swift impact, a transparent column leaps up, slowly subsides, and passes away in equally slow circles. An increase of speed proceeds parallel with the strengthening of the rain and the widening of the set-up. The huge, wide expanse of a steadily pouring network of heavy rain, and then, suddenly, the sharp introduction of a close-up of a single stream smashing against a stone balustrade. As the glittering drops leap up—their movements are exceptionally slow—can be seen all the complex, wondrous play of their intersecting paths through the air. Once more the movement speeds, but already the rain is lessening. Closing, come shots of wet grass beneath the sun. The wind waves it, it slowly sways, the raindrops slide away, and fall.' There is no doubt that this principle has exceptional powers. In moments of heightened artistic sensibility, the structure of movements becomes plain, together with the precise relation between their parts and speeds, which gives them their significance. The temporal close-up must never be allowed to degenerate into a trick. It is not an odd assortment of actions, patched together by some shallow news-reel man; it is an instrument of precision for rendering on the screen the shortest and most valuable experiences, in so far as they relate to physical movement, rather than to pattern or thought.

22. The remaining province of film-motion is reversal. If the film is passed through the projector in a direction opposite to its passage through the camera, movements on the screen will appear reversed. The most usual application of reversal is to slapstick, where the spectacle of bicycles travelling backwards is considered very diverting, as is that of the fragments of a cup lying on the ground, which will cohere, fly up to the table and reseat themselves in their normal position on the saucer. There are not many instances in serious work. Two sequences from *October* may be mentioned: the abdication of the Tsar was represented symbolically by the disintegration of an immense statue of him, from which first the royal insignia and then the limbs fell down, until only the internal scaffolding remained. When, later, the reactionary nature of the provisional government was discovered, the reverse process occurred; the descended parts bowled upwards to their places, the head swayed and settled down upon the

neck, and the image of tyranny was again complete. Where, in general, it is intended to demonstrate the restoration of what once was shattered, this is no doubt a valuable weapon; but it must be remembered in a limited field such as this that 'To-day's innovation becomes to-morrow's cliché, and the day after to-morrow's joke'.

23. Similarly, the resources of optical distortion can be used guardedly, and may be easily abused. Instances, however, are gratifyingly rare. The dismay of the bankers at the Wall Street collapse, following the unprecedented boom in which their fortunes had been made, was represented in *The Conquerors* by a sudden falling away of the lower parts of their faces; the effect, which sounds merely ridiculous in words, was exceptionally graphic in a short shot. In *Uberfall* (Metzner, 1929), the recovery of a man after an accident was shown by distorted shots of the incidents which preceded it; in *Brumes d'Automne* (Kirsanov, 1929), the despair of a woman who had lost her lover, by dim, drawn-out shots of the river beside which she wandered. The general tendency, it will be seen, is to try and penetrate into the subconscious and the fringes of the conscious by a confused mistiness and distortion of images; this, of course, has the approval of the *surréalistes*, in whose films a valuable adjunct is exalted until it dominates the whole. The splitting in half of the priest's head

in *The Sea-Shell and the Clergyman* will be easily remembered by those who, having missed the recondite allusion, found the incident merely unpleasant.

With a more orthodox use of lenses, less striking but probably more useful effects can be produced. Wide-angle lenses give a curvature to the outer parts of the camera-subject, by which attention is swept in from them and concentrated on the central area. Long-focus lenses reduce the impression of depth, and crowd objects which are arrayed behind one another into a single plane. Let us suppose that a director wished to show a massed approach of tugs up a river. Shot close to with a lens of normal focus, the result would be disappointing, the ships merely straggling up in a line from the distance. But on retiring to a more remote position, and substituting a lens of longer focus, he would find that the impressive appearance of massing was at once achieved, while, owing to the higher magnification provided, the boats would occupy as large a part of the screen as before.

24. Mechanically allied to the use of lenses is the manipulation of focus. If it is desired to shift the spectator's attention from one object to another, it is possible to avoid cutting, so long as both objects can be separately seen in the field of view, and are at different distances from the camera. The procedure can be illustrated from the best example which has

hitherto appeared. In *Der Träumende Mund* (Czinner, 1932), a violinist was playing on the concert platform, while a woman in the audience, having fallen in love with him at first sight, was watching him with rapt attention. The camera was set up just behind the violinist's left shoulder, so that his bow was visible in the near foreground. This at first was kept in focus, presumably so that the spectator should be made forcibly aware of the violinist (though indeed Beethoven's Violin Concerto was to be heard throughout the sequence). The audience was seen in a dim blur in the background. Next, the camera-focus was altered, so that the audience became sharp, and Elisabeth Bergner was clearly seen; simultaneously, of course, the violin faded into obscurity. This process was subsequently twice repeated.

The dissolve which seems indicated here (a cut might have been a little abrupt) would, it might be urged, have occupied too much time; it would at least have avoided keeping a large misty object in the foreground from which the attention was supposed to be diverted. This objection applies wherever the method applies; though slight, it has only to outweigh slight advantages.

25. Lastly, we turn to superimposition, the limiting case of which is reduplication. In the silent cinema the difficulty of conveying thoughts in the

absence of speech was sometimes overcome by fading in, on top of some part of the existing shot, a sort of medallion of a young woman pining for release from her captors, or a young man riding gallantly to a rescue. This device was universally disapproved by the intelligent critics, but its recent reappearance in *The Constant Nymph* shows that it is not yet dead; it merits examination, but as it raises the large issues of the pictorial propagation of thought, this treatment must be deferred to the next chapter. A few structural comments are in place here. The object, if any, which has given rise to the reflection must not intrude itself on the inserted shot. In one instance in *The Constant Nymph*, a letter was to be seen apparently racing across the surface of a hockey field; in *Pacific 231* the clash of 'cellos and railway engines, though intentional, was little better than absurd.

A quite distinct application of superimposition proposes to take advantage of this mêlée. Emotional or physical disturbances are often represented by a multiplicity of simultaneous shots, containing movements in constant conflict with one another, while the shots themselves loom out of the distance and, before they are clearly seen, disappear into it again. (Cf. the war sequence in *Cavalcade*, Lloyd, 1933.) This device is based on a fallacy. Just as it is not permissible for the novelist to convey boredom by boring his readers, so the director must not convey confusion by confusing his audience. The artist should aim at keeping continually alert the minds and emotions of those who are to appreciate his work. If he stuns them with the impact of his presentation, they will become numb and unresponsive; if he bewilders them, they will try to find some distinct statement where none was intended, and in the resulting incoherence of mind they will fail to attend to a succeeding passage in the work which would otherwise have presented no difficulties to them. Superimposition for this purpose ought to be abandoned altogether.

There is still another use for it, however. Pudovkin, in *Deserter*, superimposed on the detail work of riveting and hammering the ship an outline shot in fast motion of the whole ship coming to completion. The idea was highly ingenious, though it could not often be used without gaining an appearance of virtuosity. A small part of the work was used to typify an entire and complex process; but as it was impossible to convey thereby a conception of the whole, that was shown simultaneously; brevity and clearness were thus combined.

A variation on this use has lately been seen in Stuart Legg's *Telephone Workers*. To gather together at the end the various threads of the film, and impress the dependence of the individual householder with his telephone on the complex system which had been described, Legg superimposed various representative parts of the system on a shot of a row of houses. Except as a concession to unimaginative indolence, this was indefensible. Contiguities are most forcible when they are least forced; and the sight of a ghostly radio transmitting mast, many hundreds of feet high, standing in a suburban street at a precariously tilted angle, was little short of ludicrous. The process which was thus crudely materialized should have taken place in the spectator's mind, the successive images of blocks of intricate mechanism and humble suburban houses fusing mentally into a general conception of a very fine and delicate system. The co-presentation of a particular radio mast and a particular street narrowed the scope of an idea which the director was trying to make as wide as the system itself. An unsuccessful short cut was thus taken to the process of implicational montage described in the next chapter.

26. Reduplication is very often met with in early cartoons (e.g. *The Skeleton Dance*, Disney, 1930). A single series of movements is executed together by a number of precisely similar figures; the effect is then markedly superior to that produced by a single figure, though the reason for this is obscure. It is perhaps recognized in the size of music-hall choruses, which, though partly accounted for by the increased attractiveness of a greater number of legs, may also

172

be due to the enhancement of rhythm by simultaneous repetition.

We have now surveyed every class and sub-class of differentiating factors, as defined above. Minuter division is no doubt possible, but it is better that the framework shall be capable of receiving later additions, than that it should be prematurely filled out at the start.

27. Sight is therefore set aside for the time, and attention turned to sound. It may perhaps appear antiquated to distinguish sounds into speech, natural sound and music.[1] This classification has long been abandoned by acousticians, who rightly observe that some natural sounds are universally considered music (*e.g.* the song of nightingales); some are considered so by certain people (*e.g.* the hum of dynamos by the mechanically minded); while some music is considered to be a natural sound (*e.g.* some modern music by the uninitiated). These confusions may be presented in a rather more systematic manner. In the first place, the familiar scales of forms are present. Speech shades gradually from its function of supplying meaning towards noise (when the speech is unintelligible and harsh) and music (when it is harmonious); similarly, sounds grade towards music, and music, when it appears haphazard and jarring, towards sound. Secondly, agreement may

[1]Pp. 48-50 above.

173

not be reached between persons on the category in which a given sound is to be placed, one contending that certain music is no more than noise, another that a certain noise is music, a third that speech is unintelligible and therefore natural sound, while others disagree with all these opinions. To the first difficulty, it must be replied that some classification is better than none, and that a crystallization into groups does no harm as long as the really continuous nature of the phenomena is constantly borne in mind. And to the second, that analysis, if it is not to become excessively cumbrous, must presuppose agreement over the greater part of the field, leaving marginal and less important cases to be dealt with afterwards.

28. These considerations apply also to the further classification of sounds, which is assisted by distinguishing two main scales of forms. These are realistic — non-realistic and parallel — contrastive. The first scale may be divided into two sub-scales, the numerical and the intensive, and each point on either sub-scale may, with certain small qualifications and approximations, be sharply divided into a contrapuntal and a non-contrapuntal use. We shall first explain this method of classification and then proceed to exemplify it. The limit of realism is reached when numerically all the sounds heard by the audience originate, or are believed to originate,

in the locale embraced by the microphone on the set, and when the relative strength of those sounds which strike the microphone is the same as those which strike the ears of the audience. The opposite limit is set by the disappearance of every sound which so originates, or is believed to originate, other sounds, meanwhile, taking their place when necessary. The qualification *are believed to originate* is necessitated by instances like the following. It is required to record the playing of a piano by a person who in fact cannot play the instrument. The camera is so placed that the keyboard is just out of sight, and the music is post-synchronized. This sound should evidently be called realistic, since the audience firmly believes it to be so; it is included by the modification mentioned above.

We can now examine the two sub-classes in greater detail. Since sounds are for the most part not discrete entities but continuous fluxes, it may seem absurd to speak of their numerical coincidence on set and screen. But in fact the position is better than this. In the most ordinary and retrograde films, at least three different types of sound may be easily enumerated. Speech is commonly recorded realistically; sounds of shutting doors and shuffling feet are omitted, often owing to imperfections in microphone technique; and music may be unrealistically added. An increase of realism in this sense would result from recording the second item and omitting the third; a decrease by omitting the first. Here, then, are the beginnings of a scale of numerical naturalism, and it might easily be extended and refined. Intensively, one limit is set, as we have said, by an exact maintenance of relative strengths; the other limit, where the relative strengths are as different as possible, is indeterminate or is determined only by the power-handling capacities (in terms of permissible harmonic distortion) of the recording and reproducing amplifiers and their associated apparatus. Moreover, it is evident that all the numerically different sounds can simultaneously undergo intensive variation; while each sound separately can vary intensively with time. At this point the machinery of classification becomes impossibly unwieldy, making it necessary to halt at a rough intensive estimate approximated over the several distinguishable types of sound.

29. Returning then to the main realistic—nonrealistic scale, we are in a position to appreciate the contrapuntal distinction. When the source of sound is invisible in the shot, but recognized to be situated in the sound locale of the microphone, the sound is said to be contrapuntal; when visible in the shot, non-contrapuntal. Various difficulties are apparent. Thus, unless the sound source is conceived to be a point, there will be no sharp division between the

two classes, for the source may appear partly in the shot and be partly outside it. But to introduce another scale here would confuse the issue without conferring any corresponding benefits. But if the simplifying assumption is made, it raises as many problems as it settles. Thus if, in the example mentioned above, the point be placed on the keyboard, or arbitrarily among the strings of the piano, the sound will be considered contrapuntal; but from the critical point of view this is undesirable. Hence it is convenient to make some assumption about a surface plane of emission of sound from an instrument, subsequently contracting this plane where necessary to a point situated within it. But this detail is not of sufficient importance to warrant further attention.

30. In practical use, realistic counterpoint can be described very shortly, having already been associated with the name of Pabst.[1] It is by no means essential to present together with a train of sounds a visual record of their sources; sometimes this would be highly repetitious, sometimes it would introduce an undesired contrast. The essence of the method is that natural sounds are chosen so as to be complementary to their accompanying shots; and, once chosen, they are realistically recorded whether they are on the shot or off. Herr Arnheim defends this use of sound at the expense of every degree of unrealism.

[1]See p. 80 above.

The cinema, he says, though it may regard nature from a particular aspect, must never interfere with its uniformity. He thus safeguards the 'formative media' of camera-angle, delimitation, lighting, etc., which were first thoroughly examined by him. On the other hand, he undermines the justification of montage, which he treats indeed in a superficial and summary way, but does not of course wish to banish altogether. The essence of montage is its irruption of natural continuity; and no *a priori* theories of the sanctity of nature must be allowed to damage the most prized possession of the cinema. But if in this paramount respect the interruption of nature is to be permitted, there can at least be no theoretical objection to considering it in another context.

31. Having removed this obstruction, it is possible to examine the selective (unrealistic) uses of sound. And here it is convenient to introduce another scale of forms which will help to show what principles can govern the selection of sounds. The film can be used to give any degree of subjectivity or objectivity to a scene. Each point on this scale corresponds to various alternatives, for both the camera and the microphone can record in any given degree the attitude of any of the characters in the scene; both can treat the same character, or either a different one; or they can take over the attitude of the director himself. The normal visual record of a film seldom expresses

exactly the visual sensations of any of the characters it is portraying at a given moment. What we see with our eyes varies continually with what passes in our minds, even if we and our surroundings appear outwardly unchanged. Thus intense concentration of thought contracts the visual field to a few square inches, even these being often out of focus; inattention causes the eyes to roam vacantly round, so that the field swings backward and forward; moments of artistic sensibility bring heightened awareness, in which colour, pattern and detail appear marvellously distinct. To some extent the camera, when used subjectively, can represent this diversity of appearances; but, as we shall discover immediately, its possibilities in this respect are limited, so that it becomes necessary to discover fresh means for entering into the thoughts of individuals. Not their sight only, but their hearing, is affected by their state of being at any moment. Writing of the most difficult nature can be carried on in the midst of talking, shuffling feet and the sound of buses and cars; as long as thought remains fluid, these sounds will be silent. Once let a hitch occur in the argument, however, so that the mind is baulked, and the noise will filter in, becoming louder and louder. Thought is still further impeded, and the work must often be abandoned. But if a chance remark of interest is heard in the confusion, the aural attention will fasten on to it, and

179

the remainder of the noise will again disappear, just as a known face in a crowd can be followed with the eye, while all else becomes blurred. There is thus a close parallel between visual and aural attention; sometimes it is better to make sight more objective than sound; sometimes the reverse. Owing, however, to the superiority of sight over sound in rendering simultaneous phenomena, the former arrangement is as a rule to be preferred. The subjective camera, unless handled with great skill and restraint, is likely to lose its way in vague romanticism. Hence there is a strong case for free selection of sounds, the bearing of which on montage will be discussed in the next chapter.

32. The second main scale, parallel—contrastive, is much simpler to deal with. The sound factor and the visual film may be used to present or evoke different concepts and emotions, the purpose of this divergence being more fully explained in the next chapter under the title of *simultaneous montage*. Sound and sight are said to be parallel when the two parts of the total film convey only a single idea, so that the one directly reinforces the other. The question of the precise limit in this direction is difficult to determine. Mr. Clive Bell contends that two artistic media cannot convey exactly the same impressions; and if this be true, the limit will be approached asymptotically and never reached. It seems evident

that a piece of sculpture and a painting could equally convey a simple concept such as 'Force'; but the sensitive spectator would be aware also of other features, such as the relations of colours, lines and planes, which would necessarily diverge between the two media. Mr. Bell's contention thus appears to be vindicated. Sound and sight are said to contrast when they convey different impressions. Here also the limit is difficult to determine; for though the visual film might convey the concept 'Force' and the sound factor 'Lethargy', the inevitable penumbra of peculiarities attaching to the use of a particular medium would blur the opposition until it had lost its precision.

But much more important than the precise definition of extremes is the consideration of the intervening parts of the scale, in which the great majority of actual films will fall. It is clear initially that the two main scales distinguished above do not bear the close relation to one another which hasty reflection might assign them. Realism and parallelism of sound might be supposed to go together; and unrealism and contrast. A comparison of the stage play and the radio play will show that the first of these connections is false. The stage necessarily and always reaches the limit of realism, as we have defined it; but the radio play loses greatly by the disappearance of the gestures and facial expression, which in the theatre permit a continuous contrast bearing other shades of

181

meaning to the audience. The second connection is no less false.

It frequently happens that at a particular moment it is only desired to present a single strand of meaning. We have already described how the camera may give a neutral rendering of a scene while the microphone, by selection and suppression, conveys the individual attitude of some one person present; or, an extension of this, the camera does not attempt neutrality, but expresses with the aid of differentiating factors the attitude of another person. This process necessarily involves a division of attention in the spectator, and a consequent loss of concentration upon each part of the theme. If, however, it is of essential importance to emphasize one such part, every other channel of communication must be stopped. This is the case of perfect parallelism;[1] and that it is required even by the most advanced directors is shown by its frequent use in *Deserter*. The opening words of one of the platform speakers were matched with a shot of the man himself; the suave, complacent gestures of the policemen with waltz-time music; the hoisting of the workers in the last moment of the last sequence with the final triumphant strains of the march. Thus where realism, even when contrapuntal, would introduce an un-

[1]Perfect, that is, subject to the qualifications mentioned above.

desired contrast or provide an inadequate reinforcement, the director may resort to unrealistic parallelism.

Though we have pointed out that realism is not necessarily accompanied by parallelism, it must be admitted that it often fails to provide a sufficient degree of contrast. The sounds which are the concomitants of a particular action are generally so closely related to it that, though they may exhibit minor differences of tendency which materially enhance it, they do not as a rule permit any striking departure from it. An occasional example, like the heedless noises in the street which give poignancy to a personal tragedy in a house near by, should certainly be made use of; natural sound would here prove far more effective than any attempt at unrealism. Usually, however, reiteration follows realism. When it is desired, there is no further difficulty. When it is unwanted, some decision must be come to as to the relative advantages of natural sound and music in taking the place of realistic recording. Natural sounds rather than music are the common accompaniments of everyday actions. Hence if a sound is heard, the audience will attempt to fit it into a realistic scheme, and in doing so may lose a great part of its significance by imagining it to be merely fortuitous. The classic example on which argument here is based was to have occurred in *Life is Good.* Pudovkin, however, made this a silent instead of a sound film, and renamed it *The Story of a Simple Case.* A woman had gone down to the station to see her husband off in the train. Her thoughts were in a tumult as time passed away, while all that she wished to say remained unsaid. The train, though in fact still beside her, seemed to be departing as it would shortly depart, since all the value to her of its standing there was lost through her confusion of mind. In order to convey this somewhat complicated feeling, Pudovkin proposed to use as his sound the roar of a train departing into the distance. Herr Arnheim, however, criticizes this suggestion with some justice, saying that the audience would merely suppose that another train, waiting behind the one seen, had left the station.[1] Had the sound of the train been suggested by musical means, as in Honegger's *Pacific 231,* no confusion would have arisen, for no realistic interpretation would have been possible. Herr Arnheim does not seem to allow sufficiently for the context of the sequence; the audience would presumably have been prepared for the woman's emotional state, and so would have assumed a subjective motion of the train, unless assured of an objective. Nevertheless, his broad contention remains firm. Contrast, where realism is impossible, is best contrived with the aid of clearly unrealistic music.

[1] *Op. cit.* p. 267.

33. We shall now turn to give a single representative illustration of each of the three most important scales distinguished above: subjective — objective, realistic — non-realistic, and parallel — contrastive. Subjectivism in sound has never been used consistently. There was a brief instance of it in *M* (Fritz Lang, 1931), where a man sitting at a table in a café put his fingers in his ears, whereupon the natural sound (here a band) faded away, and swelled out again when he removed them. This was, of course, very ineffective, since the cessation of sound was an inevitable and therefore anticipated consequence of the man's action. A much better example occurred in *Blackmail* (Hitchcock, 1929), when a girl, having murdered an artist for the usual reason in a moment of disgust and terror, heard the words 'Knife, knife, knife . . .' leaping out of the hubbub of voices, as the crowds she walked through read of the crime. This subjective use of sound has been regrettably neglected, perhaps because of the bane of the 'highbrow' which haunts even the most advanced directors.

34. Free transposition (perfect unrealism) of speech and sound must, we have said, be applied with great care; but it need not be excluded altogether. Indeed one of the simplest uses of speech and music, the commentative (defs. B. *a*. 3 and B. *c*. 2), falls into this class. The voice which comments on newsreels or on simple lessons in natural history is never

supposed to have had any place in the sound locale of the shots being shown. This is accepted as a premise and does not result in any confusion. The proper use of such a commentary is discussed later in connection with the documentary film. There is, however, one distinct type of commentary which needs attention here. This is the internal monologue, developed by Eisenstein in connection with a script of Theodore Dreiser's *An American Tragedy*, which he was asked to write in 1930 at the time when he was in Hollywood. The film would have been an even stronger indictment of American social life and judicial practice than was the book; it was therefore taken away from Eisenstein, though approved by Dreiser, and the internal monologue was never realized. Its effect can only be judged from Eisenstein's (presumably imaginary) description;[1] he always commends his own ideas with the most single-minded fervour; and though he says here 'THE TRUE MATERIAL FOR THE SOUND FILM IS, OF COURSE, THE MONOLOGUE,[2] it seems better to give it an important rather than an exclusive place in an account of the applications of sound.

Eisenstein points out that the inward monologue as a literary form, though used first in Dujardin's *Les Lauriers sont Coupés* in 1887, was not fully perfected until the publication of James Joyce's *Ulysses*.

[1] *Close-Up*, June 1933, pp. 120-123.
[2] Capitals in the original.

Literature, however, is too confined by the restrictions of words, and drama by the restrictions of relative naturalism as well, to evoke the full force of this method. Only in the film can it be realized. It will be recalled that the first climax of *An American Tragedy* is a scene in a boat, in which a young man, goaded by the difficulties which his weakness and his social surroundings have inflicted on him, and restrained by his irresolution, battles with himself over his desire to kill the girl who is accompanying him. Eisenstein describes the script as follows.

'These montage sheets were wonderful. . . .

"The film alone has at its command the means of presenting adequately the hurrying thoughts of an agitated man. . . .

'For only the sound film is capable of reconstructing all the phases and specific essence of the process of thought.

'What splendid drafts of montage sheets these were!

'Like thought, they proceeded now by means of visual images—with sound—synchronized or non-synchronized. Then as sound—formless—or with sound images: sounds symbolizing objects.

'Then suddenly, by the coinage of words formulated intellectually—intellectually and dispassionately, and so uttered. With a black film—hurrying, formless visibility.

'Now by passionate incoherent speech. Only substantives. Or only verbs. Then by interjections. With zigzags of aimless figures, hurrying along with them synchronously.

'Now visual images hurried along in complete silence.

'Now sounds were included in a polyphony. Now images. Then both together.

'Now interpolating themselves into the external course of events, now interpolating elements of the external course of events into themselves.

'Presenting, as it were, the play of thought within the *d(r)amatis personae*—the conflict of doubts, of bursts of passion, of the voice of reason, by quick movement, or slow movement, emphasizing the difference in the rhythms of this one and that, and, at the same time, contrasting the almost complete absence of outward action with the feverish inward debates—behind the stony mask of the face.'

If this passage be read quickly, and without too much attention to the details (which only the script could clearly reveal), it will probably be admitted to show great possibilities in the direct penetration of the mind, particularly in moments of stress when logical accuracy is out of the question. It is, of course, liable to abuse: the method of *Strange Interlude*, in which the mask of social convention was removed by asides interspersed in the text, merely echoed in the clumsiest manner what the actors had skilfully conveyed. In Eisenstein's description, it should be noticed, the visual film is often subjective, attempting to represent the confused and fleeting images of bewilderment, and the blankness which closes on the mind when it is cornered by impossible circumstance. Not until film audiences are prepared to make the effort, which some of their members already make as readers of introspective novels, to translate themselves as far as possible into the consciousness of others, will some of the greatest potentialities of the film be realized. The novel is probably now too much occupied with the labyrinths of the self; it is certain that the film is not preoccupied enough.

The free transposition of natural sounds is thus applied most safely, though not necessarily most effectively, when it is intended to be objective. Thus in *Deserter* there are two sequences showing the building of a ship. The shots represent hammers, drills, falling chains and blinding flashes of light; the sounds, though taken from the actual scene, would never be heard together in any part of the ship, still less would be combined in the complex rhythm which Pudovkin imposed on them. No difficulty, however, was experienced in watching these sequences; sight and sound were highly selective interrelated epitomes of a long, objective process.

35. We turn now to some special applications of music, beginning with the simplest, which cut across the previous method of classification. Examples of the imitative use (def. B. *c.* 1) are very rare, though they occur in the opening sequence of *City Lights* and in early Disney cartoons. Pompous speech in particular can be caricatured by distorted musical sounds. Arising out of this is the commentative use (def. B. *c.* 2). Lubitsch and René Clair were the first to discover how easily the important could be reduced to the absurd, without the smallest visual misrepresentation, by a light sarcastic musical comment. This method, though often amusing, is not very profound. The truest comedy springs out of the situation itself, as revealed by the artist, and is not overlaid on it by epigrammatic remarks.

36. The evocative use (def. B. *c.* 3) can be extended until it replaces speech altogether. It depends on the emotional appeal (recognized in opera) of all music except the purest, and proposes to use it, in conjunction with the visual film, to convey every concept which the story of the film demands. It is liable to degenerate into the meaningless concoction of melodies we have already deplored; but it can on occasion be a valuable adjunct where the visual film has to be left free of natural sound accompaniment for purposes of cutting. Thus in the more tranquil passages of the film, it can indicate by the aid of

leitmotifs the tendency of thoughts which have no visible sign, or else prepare the audience for some new situation which is soon to arise. But when the action quickens, the emotive music must either strike out a line of its own (as in the contrastive functions already considered), or it must subordinate itself to a merely dynamic function (def. B. *c.* 5). It must never attempt to follow emotively the rapid changes of feeling which the director may wish to excite in his audience (*e.g.* the battle—stock-exchange sequence in *The End of St. Petersburg*). An unsuccessful attempt was made to do this in *Deserter*. The glib, mellifluous music which accompanied the capitalists as they glided to and fro in their cars was sharply interrupted for natural sound as soon as the girl who was selling strike papers appeared. On returning to the cars, however, the music was cut in again. This abrupt transition proved to be jarring, so that the effects of cutting sound were lost.

37. Dynamically, the value of music is considerable. The score should have no independent purpose, and should be as simple as possible, a single phrase or group of phrases being ceaselessly repeated in a crescendo of volume or in an increased tempo as long as a single cutting sequence lasts. The score composed by Edmund Meisel for *Ten Days*, and expanded by E. Irving for *October*, was perfectly fitted to this task. The problem of matching music to a

191

film already made is very difficult; it must neither impede the director's original intentions, nor supply comments or overtones of meaning of its own.

A further application of sound proposes to combine simultaneously the realistic use of speech with the evocative use of music. Thus, in *Extase*, a few words had been overlaid on the music, but their effect was very disturbing, since they never amalgamated with the characters but seemed to be spoken as a commentary. It seems possible to combine in the mind two distinct impressions which appeal at the same time to two different sense-organs; this is all that evocative and contrastive music demands. But with a combination of sounds which have originated in different locales, the case is otherwise; so long as one (*e.g.* the music applied to lecture-films) is content to flow in an almost unnoticed undercurrent, scarcely of any value, no difficulty arises; but, as soon as both assume importance, a feeling of heterogeneity appears and the spectator becomes dissatisfied.[1] This may only be a matter of acclimatization; but it is a step considerably in advance of the freest uses of sound we have hitherto examined.

The place of music in films is at present indeterminate and largely unexplored. It cannot be discussed with the precision attaching to the visual components, which have nearly all been given ample

[1]See p. 246 for corroboration from the visual film.

opportunity on the screen to form the basis of careful and extensive judgments. It is hoped, however, that the distinctions drawn above will promote some understanding of the functions of music and of other types of sound; fuller criticism must await further experiment.

38. It is with the bearing of all these tools, mental and mechanical, on the theme of his film, that the scenarist as well as the director is concerned. Hitherto we have assumed the two persons to be one; and though we are not concerned with the way in which work is in practice divided between them,[1] we must consider a theoretical fallacy which is perhaps widely entertained. Mr. Dalton, in an article entitled *The Misconception of 'Montage'*,[2] remarks: 'I propose to demolish it (*sc.* Kuleshov's theory of montage). Being a scenario writer, I must; for I cannot assent to a theory which makes the director the sole creative artist, and the scenarist a mere assistant.' This ingenuous confession of an interested motive in part excuses the confusion which vitiates Mr. Dalton's reasoning; but as the reasoning is stated in a somewhat disingenuous manner, it will be well to examine it in detail. Mr. Dalton very properly begins by asking 'What *is* montage?' It is, he says, an offshoot of Kuleshov's theory of composition, and 'is

[1] See Pudovkin's *Film Technique* for an admirable account.
[2] *Cinema Quarterly*, vol. i. no. 2.

backed by the great authority of Pudovkin and Eisenstein, and therefore claims the credit for their achievements'. He goes on to quote a passage from *Film Technique* which he associates with the names of Kuleshov and Pudovkin himself, and is able to demolish various statements in it with the utmost ease. After patronizingly conceding 'a grain of truth', 'a dim perception of the peculiarity of the film art', he continues: 'There is no such thing as "montage". The duties of the director, after the film has been shot, are, firstly, to select the best shot of each scene (where more than one have been taken), and secondly, to cut each shot to its correct length, which is completely determined by the nature of each shot and by its context. Both these functions need skill, experience and fine judgment; neither of them needs creative imagination. "Constructive cutting" is, of course, another mirage of similar origin.' The excellent results obtained by the Russians using a mythical method are easily explained away by the fact that they combine the functions of scenario and direction in a single person. Mr. Dalton complacently concludes: 'The Kuleshov theory, and with it the conceptions of "montage" and "constructive cutting", must be demolished. I hope I have performed the job satisfactorily.'

The inner workings of this argument are as follows. The passage quoted by Mr. Dalton is itself quoted in Pudovkin's book; this fact Mr. Dalton suppresses, and by so doing is able to foist onto Pudovkin a theory which he is the last person to hold, as is made clear in his book. The quotation is actually from Kuleshov and represents the theory he put forward in 1923. Like all attempts to gain a hearing for a truth which had never before been recognized, it had to be presented in an exaggerated form. In this form it was soon after explicitly repudiated by both Eisenstein and Pudovkin, who, however, modified and expanded it, as is clearly seen in *Film Technique*, until it showed scarcely any connection with the work of Kuleshov. It is only this very different theory, the basis of the present book, which can claim to be at the bottom of the Russian films also. Hence Mr. Dalton, by demolishing a long-abandoned theory, and associating it with the name of one who left it behind nearly ten years ago, reaches a conclusion which bears no relation to the facts.

The true position is this. The scenarist may conceive in his mind every detail of every shot and precisely determine its length, write every necessary word, lay down every natural sound or piece of music; and in that event the director is a mere mechanical executive, a manipulator of actors and properties to a given formula. Or, on the other hand, the director may dispense with a written scenario, shooting a whole film from a clear conception of it in his mind, and cutting it with the same guide. Neither of these extremes is likely to be realized in practice. The complexity of the film medium, which even at this stage will be apparent to the reader, together with the non-chronological order in which films have to be shot, demands a programme in words of the action which the director makes the basis of his work. But the film and not the scenario is the ultimate work of art; the scenarist, if necessary, is necessary only as a assistant; and even where the director disappears except as an automaton, the process of montage survives intact. Someone must do the creation; it must be filmic and not literary creation; and if it is done by the scenarist his montage can at the worst be bad; it cannot be non-existent. The use of montage may reside in one person or another, or it may be divided between them; but it is always present. The separation of scenarist and director may be considered as a frictional force impeding the embodiment of an idea in a film. The communication between the two can never be perfect, so that the finer points which might otherwise be conveyed are rubbed off and lost. Everything we said on the simplifying assumption holds good qualitatively when it is removed; but there will be a quantitative attrition unless, as should always be the case, the director writes his own scenario.

Chapter VI

Technique of the Film:
2. Synthesis

'If we examine the dialectical process in more detail, we shall
find that it advances, not directly, but by moving from side to
side, like a ship tacking against an unfavourable wind.'
McTaggart: *Studies in the Hegelian Dialectic*

1. The structure of the cinema has now been analysed to the degree proper to an introductory study. The method of *ceteris paribus* was pursued throughout; for, following a broad survey of the field, the numerous independent variables which confront the director's mind were brought to rest. The alternatives to the cut, the simplest and most abstract of these, were then released and examined; while in the field of differentiating factors, the optical and the non-optical variables, the static and the dynamic, the natural and the filmic, represented stages in the gradual complication of the problem. Finally, when the whole throng was moving together, the structural aspect of montage was related to the scenario.

Thus, starting from a set of preliminary definitions, the basic tools and concepts of the cinema have been arrayed. Certain necessary criticisms attempted to sweep the ground of previous encumbrances; but the main task was to clarify the scope and nature of the cinema's instruments of construction. The use and purpose of these instruments is our present task; and the fact of primary importance to be emphasized in this chapter is therefore the method by which the film produces its effect. We have dealt in Chapter IV with the types of film whose technique resembles that of the stage, and is to be studied in books whose concern is the stage; here, our main interest is with the peculiar properties of the film, which produce their effect in non-theatrical ways.

2. These properties, in their constructive aspect, have commonly been grouped under the term 'montage', which has for many years inflated the currency of cinema discussion, a token coin with a very nebulous backing. Montage has long been described as 'constructive cutting', 'creative composition', 'film editing', and so on; but these terms, being as obscure as the term montage itself, have failed to shed any light on it. Indeed, at the most primitive level of error, its very existence has been denied. Thus, to say with Mr. Dalton that montage is a mirage is to assert what as a scenarist he is the first person to deny, that there is no method of composition peculiar to the cinema. If the name montage is given to this method, whatever it may ultimately prove to be, all will admit it to exist in view of the numerous independent properties which the cinema possesses. But even those who have grasped this fact frequently fall into the error mentioned above of defining montage in terms which are no clearer than itself. Thus, Mr. Braun, in a leading article entitled *film: definition*, observes: 'Montage is film editing done constructively. Exactly *when* and *where* each single shot is begun and ended. In a film, a scene is meaningless by itself. When mounted, when put with other scenes, it has meaning. . . . It

is montage (constructive film editing) that is (in the words of Robert Fairthorne) *the manipulation of (this) sequence and duration to create the desired effect.'*[1] This definition, and under so pretentious a title we may expect an authoritative and carefully worded statement, is unhelpful and jejune. The maker of lecture-films, who cuts his strips of film to illustrate a commentary regulated by the exigencies of grammar and scientific description, is classed with the film symphonist, the length of whose strips is decided only by a complicated formula empirically determined, which results in the production of pure form and the emotion connected with it. The montage of both is intended 'to create the desired effect'; but in the one case it is regulated entirely by considerations of grammar and science, with no regard to the properties of the cinema; and in the other, by considerations of the cinema, and none else whatever. To define montage in such a way that it does not distinguish between these cases is as valuable as to define a banana as a beetroot and explain that both are types of food. Mr. Braun, however, is so pleased with his definition that he exclaims: 'That's why we everlastingly talk about montage and say montage

[1] *film art*, winter 1933, p. 41. Italics as in original. There is a strong resemblance between this passage and the antiquated theories of Kuleshov, left behind nearly ten years earlier.

montage montage and montage again.' This incantation proves to be no new dialectic leading up to undiscovered truths; but a mere soothing hum, lulling Mr. Braun into a belief that he is moving, when all the time he is standing still.

3. The primary structural, as opposed to analytical,[1] peculiarity of the cinema is discontinuous presentation; the primary means of producing it is the cut. Certain cinema enthusiasts have tended to regard the cut as a mysterious entity, so considerable being the power which results from a mere timeless transference, a non-existent means. It has thus seemed to them that the cut must be a new discovery, and montage an almost supernatural creative process. Others, chiefly scenario writers and those who have come to the cinema from literature, dismiss the cut as an irritating disjunction, or at best consider it a convenient substitute for theatrical scene-shifting. These, therefore, as we have seen, deny to montage any real existence.

Both views are too extreme. Cutting is as old as contrast. Latin words follow Anglo-Saxon; long and short sentences are alternated; passages of vigour and activity are succeeded by quietness and calm. In music, *piano* changes instantly to *forte*, a collision

[1] The two concepts overlap, and are thus not opposed in the manner of exclusive species, like mammals and oviparous animals.

which enhances both the previous silence and the subsequent volume of sound. The grave-diggers in *Hamlet* and the porter in *Macbeth* show that irrelevancies may be interposed to heighten effect, and that, by cutting abruptly from one to the other, the trivial may magnify the great. But this is not to disparage the superior value of cutting in the cinema. Contrast will increase in value as it decreases in difficulty. The cinema has developed the most direct and forcible of all means of contrast; it has for advantage the suddenness of pictorial onset, by which the spectator is more vividly, though doubtless less deeply, impressed than by the slow development of literary effect; and further it gains from the effortlessness of its mechanism. The more effacing the means of contrast, the more effective the contrast itself. The stage therefore rightly makes greater use of flux than of sharp antithesis; but it would be foolish for the cinema to neglect a weapon which has fallen almost perfect to its hands.

4. The consequence of antithesis is that the effect of any one shot differs sharply from that of its precursor and successor, resulting in an impact of the sensations and concepts derived from contiguous shots; and from this impact may arise a third concept different from that of either of the components which produced it. This we shall call montage. There is nothing radically new in its nature. The

man who had no knowledge of an explosion would watch with indifference the application of a match to a bomb; but, if he survived his first experience, the concept 'explosion' would immediately arise in his mind if the concepts 'match' and 'bomb' were presented to it in rapid succession. This process would normally be called *inference* or *association;* but in discussions of the cinema it is convenient to reserve to it a special word, which has the connotations of an art rather than of philosophy, and may without straining a usage be extended from the inferential production of effect to the conjunction of the visual or aural units from which effect in the last analysis arises. Montage, in various forms, permeates every stage of the spectator's appreciation of the true film. The most immediate awareness of the content of shots and the significance of sound is indeed the result of a more direct and elementary process. But the marked distinctions between shot and shot, cut and cut, sight and its coincident sound, idea and idea as they are generated parallel within the mind, or are opposed to some permanent part of its armoury of concepts, provide opportunities for montage, which is harsh and crude the more violent the collision, and subtle and penetrating the narrower and finer the distinction.

Our own definition, like Mr. Braun's, carries the matter only one stage back, and there leaves it. The processes of mental association are familiar to everyone; the laws which govern them are the province of psychologists, and it would be improper for the nonspecialist to dogmatize upon them. But just as economics cannot be upset by future advances or confusions of psychology because, starting from the same data, the two sciences proceed in opposite directions, so the theory of montage we here propound rests secure upon the same basis. Its advantage over the other theories mentioned lies in drawing attention to a fact which, though long known even in the cinema, is almost invariably forgotten. Implications have been recognized when their production was common to the other arts; but the lower montages have been ignored, or at best employed in a random or occasional manner.

5. Montage, therefore, is the mechanism of an obliquity apparent in the smaller facets as well as the larger aspects of a film; and it is in connection with obliquity that film technique and personal subject must here be shown to coincide, just as the coincidence of technique and social subject is demonstrated in the next chapter. Dr. Tillyard has recently drawn attention[1] to the fact that great works of art are in their very nature oblique. That is to say, though their parts have an explicit reference to the events which they on the surface portray, the whole which these

[1] *Poetry Direct and Oblique.*

parts compose has an indirect and implicit reference (which he calls a 'great commonplace') giving the chief value to the work of art. This commonplace is nowhere directly stated, but is everywhere implied; a concealment which is not a mere coy deception or a hankering after cross-word obscurity, but a condition of the artist's experience of the truth he is attempting to communicate. Thus, Pope's *Essay on Man* contains not one but hundreds of great commonplaces; each of these, however, is directly stated; and the reader, ignorant as he may be, can master their content, just as the poet might have written them, without proving their validity through his own experience of life. It is a commonplace of criticism to rank didactic as the lowest branch of art; which is no more than to say that the artist, where he is concerned with moral judgments at all, is directly concerned with particular selected judgments and not with general maxims. In this way, artistic expression and communication are based on a community of experience; the truth contained in oblique art, not being stated in concepts, can be apprehended only by those who have shared what the artist has felt. Dialectic, or the approach by statement, counter-statement and resolution, plays therefore an important part in artistic method. Obliquity appeals to the facets of experience and shadows out from them a philosophy of life; dialectic is the principle on which these facets are selected, so that an advance may be made from lower to higher levels of reconciliation. The dialectical process, moreover, is seen as clearly at work in the life of the individual as in that of the community. During the stages of his growth, the individual champions in turn and finally resolves all the famous opposites: classicism and romanticism, capitalism and communism, thought and action, passion and restraint. Kuno Fischer has said: 'Human life resembles a dialogue in this sense that, with age and experience, our views concerning persons and things undergo a gradual change, like the opinions of the interlocutors in the course of a lively and fruitful conversation. This involuntary and necessary change in our outlooks on life and the world is the very tissue of experience. . . . That is why Hegel, when comparing the evolution of consciousness with that of a philosophical conversation, has given it the name of dialectic, or the dialectic movement. Plato, Aristotle, Kant, each of them employed this term in an important sense peculiar to himself; but in no philosophical system has it been given so comprehensive a meaning as in that of Hegel.'[1]

6. Obliquity can be regarded from two aspects: clash or conflict, and dialectic or implication. The

[1]Quoted by G. Plekhanov in *Fundamental Problems of Marxism*, p. 123.

first corresponds to the simplest and lowest form of montage, the rhythmical, which is treated first; the latter to subtler forms which follow after. Rhythmical montage makes a powerful sensuous appeal, awaking primitive passions and activities; the higher montages stimulate the mind and the developed emotions. Rhythmical montage, being the form most susceptible to abstraction, occupies more space than its relative importance deserves; but it gives scope to a method of analysis which confers a singular clearness on some branches of aesthetic discussion, besides raising a number of questions of philosophical interest. This method is a graphical one, and it is therefore well to inquire what assumptions it entails, and to meet criticisms from those who may think it to have little bearing on the facts of experience; or, in opposition to this, to be so mathematically precise as to make the film a product of calculation, rather than of a free imagination guided by an accurate knowledge of the grammar of the art.

The spectator of a play, the reader of a book and the listener to a piece of music are aware of changes in themselves produced by these works, changes which themselves change as the work proceeds. Thus the dramatic tension of a play is said to increase or decrease, its tragic effect to deepen or become less intense, and the interest of a book to heighten or fall off. Climax and anticlimax represent peaks and valleys of effect occurring at and before the beginning of some interval; 'flat' passages denote a constant value of effect continuing over some period of time. But increase and decrease, height and depth and intensity, 'flatness' and maximum values are the mark of commensurable qualities. It is not enough to claim that one state of an emotion can be compared with another state of the same emotion; what is claimed is that feelings of anger can be balanced against those of regret, and of joy against those of jealousy. Thus, though it will never be possible to assign to such feelings units of amount, it is permissible to represent them graphically, placing time upon one axis and quantity of emotion relative to some arbitrary base upon the other.

A statement of the relation between affective tone and rate of cutting must then be given by one of the following hypotheses:

(1) That affective tone results from affective factors in the content of shots cut, and not at all from the rate of cutting.

(2) Conversely, that affective tone results solely from the rate of cutting, and not at all from content factors.

(3) That affective tone results from two interdependent factors, content and rate of cutting; and that rate of cutting, though it can produce affective

tone when combined with positive content, can produce none when the content factor is inoperative.

(4) Conversely interdependent; that content factors, though they can produce affective tone when combined with positive rate of cutting, can produce none when the cutting factor is inoperative.

(5) That affective tone results from two independent factors, content and rate of cutting; and that each is able to operate in the absence of the other.

Hypotheses (2) and (4) can be dismissed at once; for the one-act play, in which the rate of cutting is strictly zero, is patently capable of producing an effect. Hypothesis (1) can best be established or refuted by appeal to an actual example, which, if not already seen, must be visualized as clearly as possible. Eisenstein has a sequence in *The General Line* depicting two men cutting a fallen tree with a double-handed saw. It is first necessary to imagine a shot which includes the men, the saw and the tree, and continues long enough to show several movements of the saw and to make clear what the men are doing with it. This visualized shot must now be compared with Eisenstein's sequence. Eisenstein set up a camera close to one man and blocked out the other by the tree between them. The saw occupied the middle of the shot, passing from the man's hand to the cut in the tree. A second camera was placed on the other side of the tree, and its shots resembled those of the first except that the log was now lying in a different position and the previous background had disappeared. In the film, Eisenstein cut the shots of one camera to those of the other: first, a man driving in the saw on one side; then cut to the other in turn driving in the saw; then back again, until an almost physical sensation was produced of the saw flashing backwards and forwards. If this sequence proves too difficult to imagine clearly, not as a series of still photographs, but as a timed and distinct succession of actions, the reader should recall examples of the method which he has himself seen. Appropriate examples are to be found in *The End of St. Petersburg*, *Extase*, *Kameradschaft* and *The Lucky Number*.

But whether the short-cutting method is visualized for the first time or recollected, its superiority over the single shot in the contexts quoted will probably not be denied. If this is granted, rate of cutting must be conceded to be a factor in the production of affective tone, and it remains to discuss its relation in this respect to content, the factor which alone on the stage has been held operative; the examples of theatrical cutting already quoted having been obscured and diminished by their obvious relation to content.

The third hypothesis holds that, if the affective power of the content were reduced to zero, no affective tone would result. Suppose, then, that a film were made whose shots represented black squares, triangles and circles painted on a white background and cut together in cyclical order. If an audience were allowed to look for some time at these shots until they became perfectly familiar with them, and were then told that no others would be used, the basic condition of unaffective content would doubtless be fulfilled. The refutation of hypothesis (1) reveals an element of shock or surprise engendered by the transition from any shot to a markedly different successor. If it were not for this, the shot of the sawing scene as a whole would have produced as much effect as Eisenstein's sequence, which added nothing to a detailed knowledge of the action. Hence, also, the transition from square to triangle, and from triangle to circle, would produce a shock or surprise, a manifestation of affective tone which is sufficient to refute the third and establish the remaining fifth hypothesis.

It is now necessary to discover some quantitative relation existing between cutting-tone and cutting-rate. The surprise aroused by the clash of succeeding shots grows very quickly, but occupies some time in dying away. This is shown by the fact that the sawing sequence produces a cumulative effect, the excitement being progressively built up as shot follows on to shot. If surprise were to diminish as rapidly as it increases, the spectator would feel a series of merely momentary excitements, and the total effect would be no greater after the last cut than after the first. Fig. 1 makes this part of the theory

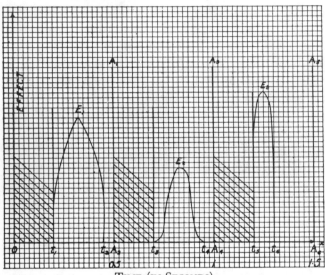

TIME (IN SECONDS)

Figure 1

clearer. The interrupted curve $t_1E_1t_2\ t_3E_2t_4$ ... represents the possibility just dismissed. Cuts are marked by the lines A_1A_2, A_3A_4, ... which give the times of cutting by their points of intersection with the x-axis. Cutting is seen to be at the rate of 120 cuts per minute. In this and subsequent graphs,

212

affective tone is not shown to increase until one-fifth of a second has elapsed after each cut. This is an approximate figure for the shortest length of shot which is able to register itself on the mind. A shorter shot therefore produces no effect at all, and hence this part of a longer shot also produces no effect.

It is reasonable to suppose that affective tone, since its zero on the graphs is arbitrary, may fall to

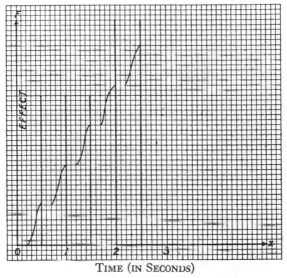

TIME (IN SECONDS)

Figure 2

this value some time after a cut has taken place. There will therefore be a length of shot for which zero affective tone has just been reached before a cut occurs and increases it again. This is the minimum length of shot which produces no accumulation of effect. If this minimum shot is now slightly shortened, there will remain a small residuum of affective tone at the cutting-point, which will be added to the amount produced by the next cut. The shorter the shot the larger this residuum will be, and the larger also the cumulative effect of cutting. Thus it is seen that cutting-tone increases with cutting-rate. In Figs. 2 and 3 an equal amount of affective tone is added after each cut, but with the result that, after four seconds, a much greater total cutting-tone is

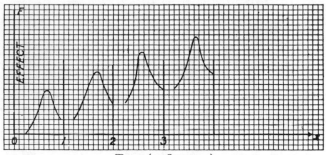

TIME (IN SECONDS)

Figure 3

produced by the half-second than by the one-second rate. There is, however, a factor which operates against the production of cutting-tone. Surprise is steadily diminished as the period of repetition occurs more frequently. Hence, after the first few cuts, the accretions of cutting-tone become smaller until they are barely able to maintain a constant total by the aid of the residua already mentioned. For this reason, if the total is to be increased, it is necessary to accelerate the rate of cutting progressively, introducing thereby a second factor assisting the production of cutting-tone.

Before this analysis can be of any service to the director, a study of content must follow that of cutting and afterwards be combined with it. The effect, or content-tone, of the material of a film is produced by a number of factors. A shot may have considerable intrinsic beauty, but little relation to the sequence which contains it; it may be highly important, but so familiar to the audience that its meaning at once becomes clear; or so allusive or apparently conflicting that its assimilation may be a matter of much greater difficulty than is warranted by its place in the film. Affective tone, here content-tone, will be produced by all the factors operating in a particular shot, and, after the first appearance of this shot, will grow to its full value at various rates. This growth also can be represented graphically. A content which is simple and striking will produce a sudden effect upon the mind. When, however, its full import has been realized, a sense of boredom will set in and, as in the case of cutting-tone, effect will diminish. If, on the other hand, the shot contains material of great intrinsic beauty, or meaning in the context of the film, its full understanding will be at-

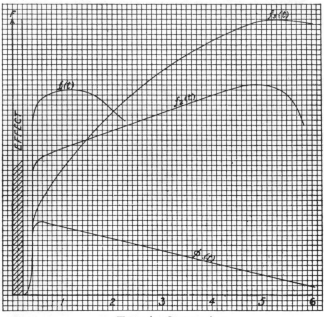

TIME (IN SECONDS)

Figure 4

tained more slowly than was that of the former shot, and the effect produced by it will be correspondingly greater. Shots of these types are represented in Fig. 4 by $f_1(t)$ and $f_3(t)$ respectively. It may appear sur-

216

prising to those who have studied paintings more closely than film shots that full effect should be shown as occurring at the most only a few seconds after first presentation; full understanding of a painting might never be reached, however long and attentively it was looked at. It is the object of the shot to be contributory, not self-sufficient. The larger wholes, from whose amalgamation the final film emerges, owe their existence to the multiplicity of the shots which compose them. Each shot therefore adds only a fragment of effect to the total—a fragment which results from its context, its content and its cutting.

The two curves of content and cutting may now be combined for some particular material. There is only one curve of cutting-tone, $\phi(t)$, for this curve relates, as was shown, to the limiting case in which the effect of the content has been reduced to zero. Its value for a given time of shot-projection, shown in seconds on the x-axis of Fig. 4 and proportional to rate of cutting, can legitimately be considered constant over any length of time for which this rate of cutting would normally be used. For we have argued that two factors operate, one in the accumulation, the other in the restriction, of cutting-tone, and that at the beginning the first preponderated, but afterwards the second. The restrictive factor takes effect more quickly in the case of short than of long shots, for it depends on a successful anticipation of the

217

moment of the succeeding cut, and is hence proportional in its effect to rate of cutting. Thus a given number of shots, whether long or short, will produce the same diminution in the increase of cutting-tone; and it seems probable that, over a fairly wide range, the accumulative and restrictive factors will balance one another. It is the resulting constant value of cutting-tone which is indicated by the curve $\phi(t)$ for a series of shot-lengths, and hence of cutting-rates. This curve can from its nature be only approximate, but it serves to show how cutting-tone increases rapidly after the first fifth of a second of projection-time, when shots can first be distinguished and seen to contrast, and afterwards falls away in the manner already shown.

The feeling aroused by rhythmical montage is by no means confined to the pure excitement which of itself it builds up. It can be conditioned by the contents of the shots whose mere conjunction produces it, and thus be made to reinforce or give urgency to these contents. Many examples of this could be given: the lorries crossing the Franco-German frontier in *Kameradschaft* (sudden determination and endeavour); the imprisoned miner hammering on a tube to attract attention, in the same film (despair and hysteria); the troop train heading for a broken bridge in *En Natt* (speed and heedlessness); sections of the crowd sequences in the early part of *Deserter*

218

(suspense). Enumeration will not exhaust the instances of such a principle, and will give little idea of its scope; these examples may, however, serve to start the mind on fresh discoveries.

To produce this simple kind of rhythmical montage, the director must cut his shots short in order to take advantage of the greatest amount of affective tone produced by cutting itself. He must also simplify and light his material so that its meaning becomes quickly apparent. The content curve will therefore rise sharply and should, as in $f_1(t)$, peak at a high value of content-tone. If the cut takes place before this maximum value is attained, the audience will feel dissatisfied that the shot has been removed before they have fully appreciated it[1]; if after this maximum, that they have already assimilated the whole meaning of the shot and are impatient for its disappearance.[2] Thus the cut must be made at the peak of the content curve.

If a dignified or tragic effect is to be secured, cutting-tone, whose effect is the opposite of this, must be reduced by long cutting. An opportunity is thereby offered for selecting material of intrinsic beauty or profounder meaning which, though it may produce a less sudden effect upon the spectator, will

[1] *E.g.* shots of buildings at the outbreak of war in *En Natt*.
[2] *E.g.* a sequence depicting telephone exchanges in *The Lodger* (Elvey).

219

attain a higher value of affective tone and move him
more deeply than did the content represented by
$f_1(t)$. An example is given by $f_3(t)$ and an interme-
diate case by $f_2(t)$.

7. Thus, to sum up the whole argument. Length
and content of shot are closely interrelated. Some
moods are best expressed and excited by quick cutting. In this event, the content of the shots cut must
be so simplified in meaning and composition as to be
readily assimilable. Other moods demand slower cutting and allow a greater importance to be attached
to individual shots. No one type of cutting must
predominate. Cuts divide sequences as well as shots,
and fast and slow cutting are each emphasized by the
near presence of the other.

It is now possible to introduce a complication into
the argument. Though, as we have said, slow cutting is as a rule necessary to produce a dignified
effect, any sort of slow cutting will be inadequate.
Cutting which is slow and irregular will merely
hamper the director's intentions; but a measured
rhythm, as in music, even though it provides little
accumulation of cutting-tone, will be of assistance.
The attentive spectator will retain in his mind the
interval between two successive cuts, which he will
then compare with the next interval; just as the
reader of the *Scholar Gypsy* carries the echo of the
rhyming word in the first line of the stanza until he

meets it again in the sixth; and the length of the expectation increases the final satisfaction. So, by a series of expectations, satisfactions and dissatisfactions,[1] the spectator can be made aware of a large number of rhythms; if the rhythms are too remote and complicated, they will seem confused and arbitrary; but practice will increase the range through which they may be profitably used.

Had rhythmical montage no other function, it would serve in this way to awake and maintain the spectator's attention. It has long been realized on the stage that variation of tempo is essential, if impossible demands are not to be made upon an audience. The most profound tragedy is not best conveyed by the slowest, even the most intense, method; it requires a speeding in some parts, in order to heighten the suspense or catastrophe of others. This is often achieved by lightening and quickening the speech rhythms, setting them off against one another, and altering the group arrangements of the characters, devices which are not applicable in nearly such a high degree to the type of film best suited to the cinema. Rhythmical montage, carrying with it corollaries of composition, is the best alternative. *October* may be cited as an example. Throughout its length of two and a half hours, it never exhausted or palled on its audience, in spite of the fact that the

[1]See Hunter, *op. cit.* p. 17, for an excellent account of this.

complicated series of events which led up to the October revolution was not of a particular interest to a foreigner, when presented with the bias of a Soviet propagandist. On the other hand, *The Wandering Jew* (Elvey, 1933), running for less than two hours, soon became heavy and dull. Both films had to lead up to a sequence which must be very slow and very impressive; the one, the terrible suspense during the negotiations in the Winter Palace between the Soviets and the provisional government; the other, the burning of the Jew at the stake. Eisenstein, however, had prepared his audience by stirring and deeply interesting them; mainly, of course, by the progress of his material on the screen, but still to a large degree by varying speeds and rhythms of cutting. His slow sequence was a complete success. Elvey, on the other hand, with every advantage in story of a personal rather than a historically distorted theme, contrived to dull his audience's attention from the start. His film moved in slow, irregular fits, so that the last sequence, though impressive by itself, fell on a numbed and unresponsive mind.

8. There is, however, another field of experiment in rhythmical montage, which may eventually prove even more fruitful than the first. The rhythm of cutting is used not to reinforce, but to contrast with the content, and to carry a separate strand of meaning. Much of James Joyce's recent prose de-

mands this simultaneous assimilation of a number of separate rhythms and meanings; the danger, of course, is that understanding becomes such a labour that enjoyment disappears. But the remedy is no less evident; the reader must be far more alert for hidden implications and conflicting sounds than he has been hitherto; and, similarly, the filmgoer must watch for cutting rhythms which convey nuances not perceptible in the more obvious elements of the film. An example of this will be given later in this chapter, where the relations of the several types of montage are worked out.

9. Leaving, then, the field of conflict, we reach that of implication. One of the most important functions of montage is to stimulate general conceptions which could not have been conveyed by purely visual means. Thus, in V. Sackville-West's poem *The Land* occur the following lines:

> *And infinite and humble are at one;*
> *So the brown hedger, through the evening lanes*
> *Homeward returning, sees above the ricks,*
> *Sickle in hand, the sickle in the sky.*[1]

So great is the power of words to evoke universals that the poet places the general statement first, and only afterwards illustrates it by a particular example. In the cinema, however, the line:

> *And infinite and humble are at one*

[1] P. 6.

is incommunicable by direct visual means; 'humble' can only be exemplified by an instance of humility; 'infinite' cannot be pictured at all. But the cinema would suffer a sad limitation were it to be restricted to particulars, from which the poet and the drama-tist can with the greatest ease adumbrate statements of universal significance.

From this dilemma there has hitherto been little escape, at least in so far as the primary elements of the film are concerned. It is true that, in the higher reaches of appreciation, the cinema is already at one with literature and drama, in principle if not in range; for implications have been discoverable in sequences of action and verbal statement, after the manner of those arts. If, however, the cinema is to be transformed along these lines into a finer vehicle of communication, it can only be by closer adher-ence to stage methods. Better acting, more revealing expression, dialogue which can compass its task by setting aside the reserves of everyday speech; all these, though they might raise the level of the screen-play, could be better applied to plays them-selves.

10. There is, however, another method, which has the advantage of leaving clear the sound factor to play an independent though co-ordinated part in the film. This is the method of primary montage; and a clear notion of it will not only facilitate the discovery

of general ideas which shots of mere particular instances can present to the mind; it will aid the con-
trivance of that conjunction of shots which in certain
circumstances achieves this aim. Thus, to revert to
our previous example from *The Land*. The approved
method of taking the scene described would be approximately as follows. The hedger would be seen
trudging along a lane, the camera tracking behind
him, so as to keep him in the same position in the
shot. As he swung his sickle by his side, the camera
would catch its shape, and, slowly panning round
into the sky, would come to rest facing the appropriate constellation. The immediate response to this
shot would be obvious; its implication would hardly
be grasped at all. If, on the other hand, a shot was
taken with fixed camera, of the sickle swinging out
as the man passed, its shape could be made the last
thing imprinted on the mind, helped if need be by a
trace of slow motion. Cut now to another static shot
of the sickle in the sky, and the spectator is presented with two clear resemblances, unblurred by
the walking man, the moving camera, the irrelevant
parts of the heavens, which were inseparable from
the normal method. The impact of the ideas of an
earthly and a heavenly sickle would now engender
an idea of general similarity, made more striking by
the contrast between the humble figure of the
hedger and the magnificence of the skies.

Countless examples could be given of lost opportunities in this field; the director has supplied a piece of dialogue or a running commentary either where a little thought would have revealed a means of montage, or where the speech merely echoed an idea which was already abundantly clear. A single instance of each of these faults may be given. In *The Private Life of Henry VIII* (A. Korda, 1933), Anne Boleyn, as she climbed the steps of the scaffold, remarked on the beauty of the day. Here there was a cut to Jane Seymour making an almost identical remark, as she continued her preparations for marriage. This childish method of pointing a simple but significant contrast blunted the effect it might have made. The forced coincidence of the two comments, and the transference between two entirely different sound locales, spoilt an incident which, devoid of its simplicity, was nothing. Had the director kept his excellent low-angle shot of Anne Boleyn mounting the scaffold, outlined against a summer sky, and then cut for a moment to Jane Seymour looking out of her window with evident pleasure on the sunlit garden, he would have produced the desired effect without any of the disadvantages attendant on the method he in fact used.

The second fault was observable in *Industrial Britain* (Grierson-Flaherty, 1933), whose purpose was to show that behind the smoke, the vast size and the mass-production of modern industry it was still the craftsman who ultimately counted. The montage here was very good. The specialist who, when machines had reached their limits of accuracy, took over the rotor of a supercharger for its final balancing; the old men, still blowing the finest pieces of glass-work, as their predecessors had blown them for thousands of years; these were shown co-operating with the intricate machines which might be thought to have supplanted them. All this was made perfectly evident by the arrangement of shots which we have tried to indicate in this brief description; but added to the visual film was a running commentary which for the most part merely repeated what had already been clearly grasped. The result was a feeling of irritation at the presumed stupidity of the audience; a better understanding of montage would have allowed any degree of obviousness in the general concept to be conveyed visually; but, by enriching the pictorial content proper to the cinema, it would not have alienated the minds which moved quicker than those for which the film was intended.

11. We have tried to show how in many cases the present function of speech can be performed pictorially. The sound factor is thus left free, enabling it to diverge and converge at different angles, to run parallel at different removes, and also to coincide with **the** theme of the visual film. The means by which

these effects are achieved have already been described;[1] but there is a further and more complicated effect which belongs to the sphere of montage.
We have seen that the contents of two contiguous
shots may have not only independent effects of their
own, but may produce a third effect which arises
from their contiguity. Similarly, a whole sequence
in the visual film may produce a single effect (in
reality, of course, a complex of content-tones and
montages); its contemporaneous sound may produce
another distinct effect; and the collision in the mind
of these two will produce a third. This is simultaneous montage; an instance may be given at once to
show how valuable to a director is a sharp and accurate conception of it.

The Rebel[2] told a story of the opposition of the
Bavarian peasants to Napoleon's invasion of their
country in 1809. The last sequence ran as follows.
The three rebel leaders, having been captured after
a defeat, were sentenced to be shot. They were stood
before a firing-squad while the sentence was read to
them, the sound being realistic throughout this part.
The squad fired, and the rebels were again seen,
fallen sprawling in the dust. But now the sound of a
patriotic song was faintly heard, ghostly figures of
the three men rose from their prostrate bodies and,

---

[1]See Chapter V, pp. 180-184 above.
[2]Part directed by Luis Trenker.

valiantly singing their song, marched at the head of the peasant forces, ascending along the rim of a distant cloud, until finally, as the song swelled to its conclusion, they disappeared into the skies.[1] The noble devotion of the Bavarians, which had previously been well conveyed, conflicted strangely with the crude conception of spiritual values revealed by the final shots; but though montage of a sort in consequence took place, it did but demonstrate the contradiction of outlook which different parts of the film displayed.

Had the principles of simultaneous montage been firmly grasped, the following method would have shown a way out of the difficulty. The capture of the rebels would have coincided with the first faint strains of the marching song, which would have increased in strength while the men were led out to die and the firing-squad trained their rifles upon them. As they fell to the ground, the song would rise to its climax, seeming to come from a great concourse of Bavarian peasants, and the film would end. First, to remove an initial objection: where the action is so familiar and clearly understood, there is no need of natural sound; the reading of the sentence of

[1] See also the end of *The Three Musketeers*; and of *The Mystery of Life*, wherein a number of nude figures, decorously fuzzed, were to be seen propelling one another along a rocky path, scrambling upwards to a Humanist Heaven.

death in an audible voice, the noise of muskets raised to the firing position, and the final roar of their discharge, were all anticipated and produced scarcely any effect. Hence the benefits of simultaneous montage would have been practically a clear gain; for the contrast of the ignominious decline of the rebellion, and the total failure of its leaders, with the increasingly triumphant strains of the song, would have evoked with the utmost brevity and force the other contrast of a people at present and by weight of numbers defeated, but unbowed in spirit to Napoleon, cherishing the memory of their heroes, and ready to lay down their life for the freedom of their land.

Whenever two separate and therefore contrasting issues are to be presented together, this method offers itself to the director. The research and experiment which were devoted to the silent film are now seen not to have been wasted; for they were largely directed at discovering visual counterparts to sounds, so that the absence of the sounds themselves should not be regretted. Simultaneous montage is the co-presentation of two entities: a silent film, built in the proper manner to provide primary, rhythmical, implicational and ideological montages, and to dispense with sound; and a sound score, composed of speech, natural sound or music, having an independent existence. These entities, though analytically they may be separated with advantage, are complementary and must be conceived together by the director.

12. Secondary montage needs no illustration, since, as will be seen from the chart, its components are the products of the lower types of montage already described. We pass, therefore, to implicational montage, which is a slight but useful extension of primary montage. The former concerns the generation of a third concept out of two concepts derived from successive *sequences;* the latter from successive *shots*. The suggested emendation of a sequence from *Henry VIII* was thus an example of primary montage, for it was simplified to two shots; the theme of *Industrial Britain*, of implicational montage. Further instances of these two types may be given to illustrate their similarities and differences. In Basil Wright's film *The Country Comes to Town* there was a very short shot of a rabbit nibbling something on the ground. The next shot showed a number of women stooping over some plants in a field and tying them up. This was a perfect elementary use of primary montage to compress expression. Rabbits nibbling are invariably associated in the mind with lettuce. The concept 'lettuce' arises from Shot 1 and is carried over to Shot 2, where the women are now recognized as tying bundles of lettuce, though this was not visible at the distance from which the shot was taken; the montage was confirmed by the mean-

inglessness of Shot 1 except in this precise connection. The indirectness of the method used made this small incident much more vivid than the normal close-up would have done; the implied is nearly always more forcible than the explicit.

In the same film a good example of implicational montage occurred. The opening sequence depicted a party of hikers standing on the brow of a hill looking at the view. The succeeding shots showed an expanse of quiet, patterned fields, a stretch of waving grass, the feeding of hens in the farmyard with food leisurely scattered from a bowl. The next sequence opened on a modern chicken-farm, where the hens were checked and registered with scientific precision. They still scrambled for their food, however, as they had been seen doing under the old conditions. The sequence continued by showing modern methods of flower-growing, and of cress- and dairy-farming.[1] By montage alone, and without assistance from spoken or written word, the following ideas were conveyed by this short and simple succession of shots. The hikers saw only the romantic beauty of the countryside, and imagined it to be proceeding now as it had for many hundred years, slow and peaceful and remote from the busy concerns of industrial life. But in fact this is totally untrue. The

[1]This account has been simplified for shortness, and does not do justice to other ideas which the passage conveyed.

country works in the closest co-operation with the town. Science urges on the hens (as an aside; they are ignorant of their place in the system, and lead the same domestic lives); it regulates and cleanses the production of milk; it turns the farmhands into skilled operatives; it does not kill the romance of the country, but places beside its poetic qualities the rigour of efficiency.

13. We come now to ideological montage, which is the last, as it is also the most difficult type of montage to illustrate; not because examples are less frequent, but because the individual's ideology varies so much with differences of class, political opinion and religious belief, that a concept which will provoke from one person a violent montage will slide smoothly into another's framework of ideas.

Alexander Room's film *The Ghost that Never Returns* opens on a prison in a mining town in an unnamed South American state. Shots of a monotonous and miserable chain of prisoners, and of armed guards incessantly shadowing and harassing them, are interposed between titles exhibiting words such as 'Humanity', 'Justice' and 'Culture'; while the prison building itself is shown to be laid out on modern and scientific lines. The meaning is clear: the South Americans use the pretence of perfect prisons with which to placate the outside world, and screen their barbarous persecution of the revolutionary members of the mining colony behind a show of kind consideration.

The effect of this sequence was not at all what the communist director can have intended. It is part of the ideology of most educated persons that the Soviet prison system is one of the most advanced in the world, and that visitors who are shown it in action are greatly impressed by its excellence. Room, however, by so clearly demonstrating how good communists may be persecuted under the specious plea of humanity, has also demonstrated how, under the same specious plea, the same fate may befall their brethren in Russia, if their labours for the common cause are a trifle too zealous or not quite zealous enough.

14. Having thus surveyed the several types of montage, we can proceed to an example in which all take part simultaneously. We shall select a film for emendation which has been widely and recently seen, so that the task of visualization required of the reader is made as easy as possible. *The Emperor Jones,* taken from Eugene O'Neill's play of the same name, described the upward path to success and subsequent downfall of an American negro. Ruthlessly pushing aside the people who had helped him, as soon as they had served his turn, he rose from the position of pullman porter to become emperor of a small island, where he was able to give rein to his

insatiable desire for display and tyrannous power. After a time, as he had anticipated, his subjects rebelled; but he had made secret arrangements for a sudden departure, and started with complete confidence to put them into practice. The rebels, however, were determined to capture him, and to this end they beat a large drum in slow, monotonous rhythm to accompany him, though far away, as he passed through a forest to the sea.

Here began the last and most important sequence, which ran for more than fifteen minutes. It was initially marred by a yellow-green coloration of the film (supposed to indicate moonlight), and a forest of the most unconvincing artificiality; so that, in the words of a critic, it resembled 'a conservatory in a second-rate hotel'. But these were minor blemishes compared with the faulty technique employed. The purpose of the sequence was to show the negro's gradual descent from the pride of the imperial uniform and majesty to the cringing terror of a savage. Past incidents in his life haunted his mind: the game of dice at which he had killed his friend, the chain-gang he was condemned to work in; and he sought escape from these memories in recalling the Baptist church which he had attended in his early years. Each of these memories came to life in a small medallion, set in the middle of a bush or in an apse of the forest. The emperor recoiled in terror, and

dispelled them only by firing at them the bullets reserved for his pursuers. The effect of this device was
ludicrous, the mind being suspended half-way between the actual forest and the imagined incidents;
the former faded into unreality, but the latter failed
to acquire the body which had struck fear into the
emperor.

Compare this with the method of montage. It is
necessary to keep the visual film intact so that it may
produce the greatest possible effect unassisted. To
this end, the emperor should have been shot from a
low angle at first, when he strode proudly into the
forest, leaving his kingdom as he had entered it. But
when insidious doubts and fears began to attack him,
the camera should have mounted higher and higher,
until from the tops of the trees it looked down on his
miserable insignificance as he darted here and there
in mindless panic. The camera should descend only
to face up the trunks of these same trees, in order to
express the size and mystery which at first overawed
and then overwhelmed him. These ideas, of course,
would arise by primary and implicational montage
from fixed shots cut together. As the sound factor is
soon to be fully employed unrealistically, it is necessary to find a counterpart in the visual film for the
monotonous beat of the drum which, with its savage
associations, slowly undermined his arrogant confidence. This is the place of rhythmical montage. The

shots which we have just described must be cut to an almost uniform steady rhythm, quickening slightly when fears began to grip him (here simplifying the material), and slightly slowing down as he was comforted by a momentary reassurance (and here material of greater significance could be used).

Passing now to simultaneous montage, we find the sound factor clear of naturalistic intrusions. Hence the clicking dice, the crash of axes wielded by the chain-gang, the chanting of Baptists, could be given their full values, mounting in strength as the emperor passed into the savage under the burden of his recollections. The contrast between these real, deliberate sounds, the empty silence of the forest, and the negro's distraught excitement, would far exceed the effect produced by a rapidly soliloquizing figure, gesticulating at the misty shape of a man standing in a bush. At the end of each subjective incident the revolver shot would force home the pitiful confusion which thought to kill ghosts with bullets. The shot might seem at first to occur in the real world which was being heard, were it not for the sight of the revolver pointed at the vacant trees and the sound echoing inanely away.

Lastly, the whole sequence would be founded on ideological montage; for it is the knowledge that the negro desires passionately the comforts and power of civilized life, but hides the primitive even closer below the surface than we do, which accounts for Jones's lust for splendour and command, and his sudden pathetic downfall to an animal's death.

15. There are several factors at the disposal of the director which are adverse to the use of montage. These factors, most of which were described in the last chapter, affect the possibilities of montage in differing degrees, and will be described in ascending order of importance; while the several types of montage are also differently affected by each of these factors. To lessen the complexity of the discussion, it must suffice to say that the lower montages in each case suffer more than the higher, so that the result of employing the adverse factors is to draw the cinema closer to the stage. True films, *by definition*, are those which abjure stage methods wherever the cinema offers a substitute from its own arsenal of properties. The question whether the play is better than the screen-play has been discussed in Chapter IV; the question whether the true film is better than the play (in the sense of being a richer and finer medium of expression) must be left to the future to decide. But even if the answer should ultimately prove negative, that cannot be assumed to-day; and directors have a responsibility to explore every resource in their own field before they borrow from others. Hence, it is as exceptional weapons that the adverse factors must be considered; they will only be

justified where the higher montages they effect (being common to stage and cinema) greatly outweigh the lower montages (peculiar to the cinema) which they efface. That subject, or treatment of a subject, is best suited to the screen in which the adverse factors are most successfully subordinated.

16. Perfect realism of sound is practically incompatible with deliberate rhythmical montage; only by the rarest accident will the dialogue in fifteen or twenty shots exactly coincide in length with the shots determined for a different purpose. Nor can it be urged that the dialogue must merely be kept short enough to offer no impediment to independent cutting: in the first place, pauses cannot be left at the end of sections of speech without good reason; and secondly, rhythmical montage often demands shots held on the screen as little as one-fifth of a second, far too short for intelligible speech. Realistic counterpoint, on the other hand, is quite compatible with rhythmical montage, and indeed the two are combined in the strike-meeting sequences of *Deserter* already referred to. *A fortiori*, the still freer uses of sound impose no restriction. Next, a greatly enhanced degree of apparent solidity will stultify every type of montage (though in different degrees) by rendering the transition from place to place too abrupt to be tolerated; the spectator will seem to have been shifted bodily. The extent of this objec-

tion depends, of course, on the amount of apparent
solidity assumed. Alternatives to the cut will always
weaken, and probably destroy, rhythmical montage;[1]
but on rare occasions they will strengthen primary
montage, particularly if the dissolve is intelligently
used. The wipe is almost always futile.

17. We have seen in the last chapter that the
value of these three factors—realism of sound, solidity and delayed transference—is only occasional, so
that they offer no impassable obstruction to the lower
types of montage. There is, however, a factor of the
utmost importance in this respect, which brings us
to a crucial choice. This is camera movement. We
have already seen that the mechanism of attention
cannot be simulated by moving the camera; and the
more movement is permitted in other connections,
the less feasible will the lower montages become; for
the smoothness which accompanies the former must
replace and not reinforce the abruptness demanded
by the latter.

The most notable uses of the moving camera have
been in fields where the competition of the stage was
not to be feared. In particular the work of Pabst,
when F. A. Wagner controlled his camera, abounded
in moving shots. They were as a rule explained by
Pabst's desire to carry over a movement from one

[1]Only three dissolves, and no wipes, are to be found in the
whole of Eisenstein's work in the silent cinema.

shot to another, this being more easily achieved by perfect continuity in the camera than in the material; and they were justified by his ability to work up suspense in gradually approaching some important object and in maintaining interest in a protracted series of similar actions. The first of these characteristics was exemplified in *Kameradschaft*, where there was a long tracking shot through a gallery of the mine. At first all was silent; but a flickering, crackling sound became steadily more audible until the camera, rounding an outwork of coal, came upon the burning gas-vent which was soon to lead to the destruction of the mine and the entombing of the miners. The second characteristic was discoverable in the earlier sequences of *Westfront*, where the camera followed a column of men approaching the front line trenches, which were under fire. Any section of their passage resembled any other, and could have been used to typify the whole. But by moving the camera parallel with the men, the spectator was drawn into their surroundings, and felt himself being driven on, as they were being driven, to suffocation underground and death.

These two cases may be generalized somewhat. The first creates a mood of anticipation, which will only fail to be aroused if the method has been repeatedly used to lead up to a fictitious excitement. This, of course, is normal in the commercial cinema,

where almost every camera movement would be
better abolished, necessitating a complete recasting
of the theme and treatment in terms of the cinema
rather than the stage. Even this restriction might
not goad the studios out of their plagiaristic habits;
for when early sound equipment demanded a fixed
camera, plays were still reproduced, but in a way
which was far more lifeless and enervating than the
competent screen-play.

In this first case, the material is stationary, while
the camera moves; in the second, camera and material move together. This provides an opportunity of
identifying the spectator with moving persons. In
the May Day celebrations in *Deserter*, and the army
setting out in *En Natt*, the camera faced the head of
the column from a low angle, and moved backwards
so as to keep the composition constant. There was
thus an implicational montage of moving exultantly
forward with the marching men. Had the required
montage been the feelings of those whom the army
left behind, another procedure would have been
followed. From a fixed position beside the line of
march, the troops would have been seen coming up
and passing the camera. Before the end of the column was in sight, there would be a cut (a pan would
incorrectly reproduce the mechanism of attention) to
a similar shot facing the departing men. Just before
the next cut, the last file would pass the camera and

recede. If these two shots are visualized, they will be recognized to give a feeling of departure, which the moving camera could not so easily achieve; and the opposite is true of the first example. In both, an implicational montage is secured; and, unless there is a montage as definite as this, the camera should be kept fixed. To fall into stage methods, facile because they borrow where they should originate, is so easy that every security against it should be taken. The cut guards rhythmical montage, the fixed camera primary montage; the director who often dispenses with them professes an independence of the nature of his medium which only the greatest artists can safely afford.

18. The last and most important factor adverse to montage is abstraction. The cinema is in the position of a very early language in its inability to convey directly more than a particular instance. It is true that plots and characters can be presented in such a way that they imply a typification of some extensive class of phenomena; while an important function of montage, as we have seen, is the provision of a marked, and sometimes a high, degree of abstraction. But a point is eventually reached where the difficulties of effecting a montage which will convey a given idea outweigh the disadvantage of employing adverse factors. Sometimes this point is quickly reached. 'Three years passed away', and 'X's cottage

was five miles from Y's' can only be conveyed pictorially in the most laborious way. Abstraction must therefore be reduced to manageable proportions by a choice of picturable incidents out of which the necessary implications can be constructed; and terms like 'frequently', 'long after' and 'far off' must be avoided in the construction of a scenario. When all such precautions have been taken, and the resources of montage, music, sound and the simile fully exploited, there may well be situations which they cannot satisfactorily explain, or could explain only with an expenditure of time which would destroy the unity of the film. Such situations will arise only infrequently in the type of film which a hundred indications have already shown to be best suited to the cinema; but their existence cannot be ignored.

19. We have seen that a very large amount of speech is not permissible because of the dangers of the stage (if it is naturalistic) and of the lecture-film (if commentative); and a very small amount of speech is equally detrimental, because it refuses to amalgamate with the characters who are supposed to speak it. Two possible solutions are available. Either speech may be confined to a few sequences, throughout which it is recorded naturalistically; this was done in *Deserter*. Or it may be used commentatively to introduce sequences which are rendered self-explanatory by it, or to bridge gaps which cannot

244

conveniently be portrayed pictorially. With the first of these two main cases we are not further concerned; it provides opportunity for displaying great skill in counterpoint, but the principles on which it is based have already been sufficiently explained. Some examples of the use of a commentary may, however, be profitably given. We have seen, in connection with certain E.M.B. films, how easily it is misused; there every detail and implication is painstakingly explained in words of one syllable, forgetful of the fact that true art sprouts ideas in the mind; it is not planted there full-grown. In *Roadwards*, however, it was plain that within the brief limits of two reels,[1] it was impossible to present pictorially the relations subsisting between the several units in the factory. A commentator, therefore, introduced each sequence with a mention of the place of the process it described in the whole system; the sequence then ran its course to a musical accompaniment, and no voice disturbed the montages.

Again, the recent proposal to film the *Odyssey*[2] could best be undertaken with the aid of a narrator. The bulk of the story would no doubt be transcribed as a sound film without speech; but necessary details of place and time, particularly in periods of transition between episodes, would need the help of

[1] Reel = 10 mins. (approx.).
[2] See *The Times*, March 9, 1934.

speech and verbal narrative. To accompany them, the visual film would be consciously subordinated, and could consist on each occasion of the same sequence, in the manner of Homer's own stock epithets and repeated lines. As epic may well prove the best source of material for the true film, so short passages of narrative linking long sequences of sound film may prove its best method of execution.

20. The director must constantly aim at the elimination of words. Not before pictorial montage and the simultaneous montage of sounds have failed, will he resort to speech; only when speech has failed, to titles. Titles are certainly the worst method of expressing general conceptions and relations. We have seen that speech will break up the homogeneity of the sound factor; but as sound, except in the abstract film, is almost always of inferior importance to sight, the effect of speech is less harmful than the effect of titles. For a sudden break into another, a literary, medium forcibly interrupts the continuity of the primary element in the film, the pictorial. Only in exceptional cases are these disadvantages offset. This will sometimes occur when the titles can fulfil a partially pictorial, as well as literary, purpose. Most commonly this is achieved by expanding titles, which, though remaining of course in the plane of the screen, seem to be rushing towards the spectator; they create an impression of a sudden crescendo of

excitement. When a single title would prove too lengthy, its contents may be split up between a succession of titles interspersed by shots. If this is carefully done by the director himself, it may form part of any concurrent rhythmical montage he has in mind; while if the words are carefully chosen to contain elements of surprise, primary montage also may occur. As a rule, however, the title is a mere obstruction to the pictorial continuity and easily falls into an echo of montage, as was the case in *Contact*. Mr. Rotha, who was at one time a firm supporter of the use of titles, seems to have demonstrated conclusively their narrow limitations.

21. Speech and titles, then, are the consequences of the employment of certain adverse factors, which are sometimes necessitated by the inadequacy of montage; but montage can be helped to prevail by increasing the divisibility of film material. Indeed the lower montages demand a considerable disintegration of material to bring them into effective use. If a dialogue between two persons alone in a room is to be rendered, the visual film will almost always become subordinate to the sound factor. This is because the range of material illustrative of the conversation is slight, being confined as a rule to the faces of the two speakers, with occasionally an important object of reference in the room. For if picturable objects outside were to be discussed, it would

be better to suspend the dialogue and relate a descriptive sequence to the speaker. Sometimes, however, the dialogue is essential, and couched in terms so abstract that there is no alternative at first sight to perfectly realistic speech. It is here that the visual simile enters the field.

Early languages had a power of abstraction and generalization as limited as that of the cinema; for though they possessed a small number of words of universal significance, where the silent film has none, they were deprived of the principle of contiguous obliquity in which the cinema greatly excels. To remedy this defect, the primitive poet had recourse to the simile. Observing that there were some phenomena, such as children laughing, or woods in spring, which frequently moved the onlookers with pleasure, and others, such as storms and wild beasts, which affected them with fear, the poet introduced them as comparisons with his characters, painting a vivid picture so as to excite as intensely as possible the emotion which he was trying to reawake from a past experience. A close analysis in general terms (after the manner of the modern novel) was outside his range of expression; but he compensated the deficiencies of language, and provided a measure of generality, by means of the simile.

The resemblance of the cinema to the early state of a language shows how valuable an adjunct the simile should be. Not only do pictures stimulate the imagination with a rapidity and vividness beyond all power of words to do, but the simile supplies the amply divisible material with which the cinema dispenses only to relapse towards the stage. An example may be given. It will be recalled that, in the Fourth Book of the Aeneid, Dido implores Aeneas to stay with her, while he, half-ready, half-loath to go, is prompted on by the gods. Virgil, while giving the several speeches which passed between Aeneas, Dido and her sister Anna, reinforces them with the following simile to illustrate Aeneas's state of mind:

> *ac velut annoso validam cum robore quercum*
> *Alpini Boreae nunc hinc nunc flatibus illinc*
> *eruere inter se certant; it stridor, et altae*
> *consternunt terram concusso stipite frondes;*
> *ipsa haeret scopulis et, quantum vertice ad auras*
> *aetherias, tantum radice in Tartara tendit.*[1]
>
> *Aen. IV*, 441-446.

The film director, like the poet, is concerned with the relation of the multiple aspects of the simile to the multiple aspects of Aeneas's character. The smaller branches, twigs and leaves of the oak sway-

[1](Paraphrase) Like the oak, strong with the strength of many years, and beaten hither and thither by contending blasts, which shriek in its branches, strip its leaves from their stems, and hurl them on the ground below. But the oak itself cleaves fast to the rocks, and pierces as far down towards the regions of Tartarus as it stretches up into the windy skies.

ing in the gale represent the outward parts of Aeneas's character which are visibly moved by the entreaties of Anna and Dido; while the strong fixity of the larger branches and trunk represents the firm resolve which drives him on past the temptings of his weaker nature to fulfil the tasks which the gods have set him. The quantity of material needed by the cinema is here available: the tree itself, other trees beaten to the ground like weak men; the trunk, main branches, leaves and twigs of the oak; its height stretching up into the sky, and its roots striking everywhere into the ground and firmly grasping and cleaving to it. Shots of all these are to be built up into sequences showing now the weaker and now the stronger parts of Aeneas's character gaining the mastery, while the musical themes, in illustration of this, compare also the crying of the wind (*it stridor*) to the prayers and tears of Anna.

The words of the disputants belong to the stage; the inadequate material of their faces to the screen-play; the visual simile to the true film. Two aspects of the simile may be enlarged on. In the first place, it is important that irrelevant or contradictory elements be eliminated. By Virgil's time the simile had much degenerated from its original function, and tended to become a mere ornament to the main narrative, contributing only the inessential beauty which illumination gives to manuscript (cf. Matthew

Arnold's *Sohrab and Rustum*). It was therefore of little account that Virgil drew attention to the leaves of the oak stripped off by the gale, falling broadcast to the ground; though this detail tends to weaken the point of the comparison. But when there is no dialogue to correct these false impressions, everything shown must be directed to the purposed end, or the spectator will rapidly become bewildered.

22. In the second place, it must be remembered that the pictorial cinema cannot describe relations except within the bounds of a single shot, a consideration which is of much importance in giving warning of the danger of close-ups becoming unrelated to one another, and of incidents losing the relative position in time which alone can make them intelligible to the spectator. Before, after, between, behind, like, different from—all these terms, which form the structure of literary description, are debarred from the cinema. This indeed is the condition of filmic space and time. Elton, in his *Shadow on the Mountains*, has a medium shot of a gardener looking at some plants in a pot. He wished to cut in a close-up of the man's hand; but finding that he had failed to obtain the necessary material in Wales, he introduced a shot taken in London. The spectator, of course, thought that the gardener was himself handling the plants; but had spatial relations been determinate between shots, it would have been

evident that the face and hand were not a yard, but two hundred miles, apart. In this respect the property is a convenience, but in regard to the visual simile it is often a nuisance. We have already seen how Pudovkin's metaphor in sound could be mistaken for an actually departing train;[1] in the same way, the visual simile or dream may be supposed a continuation of the naturalistic narrative. Thus, in *Hunted People* (Feher, 1933), a hungry child sleeping with his father among some tramps by the seashore imagined them to be throwing him large fishes full of meat, which he devoured with enjoyment. It seemed at first, however, that this was taking place in the actual world, instead of in the child's disordered mind; the sequence, indeed, was shot in slow motion, but a director enterprising enough to shoot it at all might well have shot it slow in order to express the reality and purposefulness of the tramps' kind action, as it appeared to the child. Again, in *Deserter*, the hero had a dream of his comrade killed in Hamburg, beckoning him to return in order to renew the struggle. The sound consisted of a woman singing, which seemed to belong to the dream until Renn got up, banged on an interior door and shouted to his neighbour to be quiet.

23. These difficulties arise because there is no pictorial method of explaining in what relation to

[1]See p. 184 above.

objective events the events described are standing; and in the visual simile there is no word for 'like'. Thus it might be supposed that the oak in the example given was merely a particular oak in Dido's garden; perhaps Aeneas was thinking how delightful it would be to escape the feminine prayers and hysterics which beset him, and wander at peace in the woods. In this way, the spectator's mind would travel far along the wrong lines; the montages would contradict one another and remain incomplete, and the whole simile would break down. There is therefore some reason to consider the possibility of inventing a pictorial sign for 'like' and obtaining agreement and recognition for it. The use of slow-motion or of fades and dissolves is out of the question, because it would deprive the director of these devices except at the beginning of similes, a loss too great to be contemplated. One device, however, has the requisite qualities, though we have often had cause to decry them in their normal application. This is the wipe. Its general purposelessness, the extreme rarity with which it can properly be used, exactly fit it for this task. Moreover, if there are a few types of wipe, such as the vertical or horizontal, which the director might occasionally wish to use, there are many others, such as the diagonal and fan wipe, which are of no conceivable value. One of these should be agreed upon as the introduction to the simile, the equivalent of 'like'; it would of course entail a disadvantage compared with the cut as a means of transition between shots, just as much in a beneficial position at the beginning of a simile as in the normal sequences where we have already found it in this capacity redundant or harmful;[1] but, as this loss would be confined to a single instance in each simile, it would certainly be far outweighed by the benefits of clearness which it would confer. We conclude, therefore, that visual similes are of great importance to the cinema, in dispensing with dialogue and providing material of sufficient divisibility to form the basis of complex montages; but that confusion tends to arise unless the simile is marked off from the temporal sequence of the narrative; and that this function is best undertaken by an otherwise worthless wipe.

24. We are now in a position to enumerate and classify the various elements which contribute structurally to the expressiveness and synthetically to the appreciation of a whole film. At the outset, the contents of individual shots will be taken as unanalysed data. The observer must then evaluate the primary, implicational and ideological montages by which different aspects of the total effect were produced.

[1]Cf. lotteries and Sunday cinemas, which, if condemned on moral grounds, cannot be condoned by allotting a part of their proceeds to charity.

He must mark the simultaneous montage which arose when conflicting issues were presented together, and must notice when the alignment or resolution of the issues caused this type of montage to disappear. He must also recognize rhythmical montage as a deliberate element in construction, conveying a meaning not only definite, but often different from that of either the simultaneous succession of shots or of sounds. Visual similes are to be remarked and related to the persons whose characters they are supposed to illustrate. Note must be made of seemingly irrelevant incidents, in case they have a temporarily hidden significance; but contradictions, as distinct from conflicts, within the simile or in its outward relation, are to be guarded against. They show a failure of imagination or attention either in director or spectator. Titles are to be criticized as likely to be superfluous, but their pictorial as well as their literary value is to play a part in the balance of merits.

Penetrating now into the shots themselves, the spectator must distinguish the manifold divisions with which the last chapter was concerned. Each differentiating factor is to be resolved into its various classes and sub-classes, so that lighting, superimposition, use of the camera and so forth, are appreciated and criticized separately and in relation to one another. The sets and costumes are to be appraised for their historical accuracy, their finish and their assistance in the composition of a scene. Lastly, it is proper to investigate the mechanical methods by which particular effects were produced: back projection, the arrangement of shadows, and the selection of lenses of differing focal length may be cited from a host of instances in this class.

Such formidable demands on the observer require some explanation of how they should be met, and some good reason for meeting them at all. It is evident that the inexpert filmgoer will be harassed and perplexed if he attempts to take stock of all the components we have mentioned; any extra benefit he might derive would be far outweighed by his tiring labours on the film, and the division of attention, which, in trying to be extensive, would merely succeed in being shallow. True as this is, it does not tend in the least to show that the most penetrating attention is valueless; indeed, we have already argued that the reverse is the case,[1] and nothing more need be said here on this subject; what is evident is that appreciation must proceed slowly from point to point, and may be valuably guided by a knowledge of what is to be looked for.

The 'film as a whole', the ultimate basis of criticism, must not be imagined as a superior entity, like the fascist's conception of the State, or the deist's of

[1]See Chapter I above.

God; it is a mere construct from its elements and cannot be apprehended apart from them. If, therefore, the spectator has let slip some vital parts of the film, his apprehension of the whole will be correspondingly less rich than was the artist's. For the artist, at least ideally, controlled every separate factor at his command, using each in such a way that it expressed most subtly or forcibly the view which he was trying to communicate. No assumption is made here, except that communication is an indispensable objective of works of art; what is communicated may differ as widely as a moral message, significant form or the life story of a piece of moss. Hence the spectator will only establish perfect contact with the artist[1] if he is aware of each detail in theme and technique which the artist made a vehicle of communication.

The procedure of appreciation therefore begins as follows. The spectator, inexpert at first, watches the film with as much intelligence and sensibility as he can bring to it. In the passages where the theme, or intellectual and emotional narrative, is most intensive, he will be least able to mark the technique and technicalities by which parts of the effect are produced. But when the theme weakens, he will find that he has a surplus of attention which he can pro-

[1]Cf. Mr. Fry's analogy of the radio transmitter and receiver, *op. cit.* p. 35.

fitably direct to these matters. As he continues to watch films in this way, his powers of insight and discrimination will increase, and may be further illustrated at a higher stage of his progress.

He is now able to take in the full import of the three channels of communication: sight, sound and rhythm of cutting. Within the shot, he weighs up the interrelated differentiating factors, noting that in one place composition has been marred by misplaced lighting, and in another that the camera has tracked or panned an unnecessary distance. Thus, even in a bad film, the spectator's attention need never wander; he can mentally reconstruct a shot or sequence in order to bring it closer to what he conceives to be the mood or instruction it seeks to convey. At the same time, his mind must be alert to seize the implications of different related passages, and to guard against such ideological montages as arise from unthinking prejudice or predilection. Finally, if the film is acted, he must judge the quality of the acting, and criticize the speech accompaniment, just as he questioned the value of each example of simultaneous montage in the other type of film.

All these processes need not take place at the same seeing. By successive doses, the tyro can gradually assimilate nearly as much as the connoisseur; but to successive applications of the film there will accrue successively smaller rewards, until finally the dissatisfaction of going to see it, and looking at what was already known, exactly balances the satisfaction of completing the remaining montages and observing the remaining relations between the differentiating factors. This is the optimum point for deciding not to see the film again; but it is improbable that an exact balance will be struck, owing to the impossibility of applying the whole film to the spectator in infinitesimal doses.

If a film is looked at in this way, it is probably immaterial how it is appreciated; that is to say, at the first seeing attention may be concentrated on the theme; at the second, on the technical ability of the acting; at the third on the various montages, and so on; or, on the other hand, it may be distributed in varying proportions over all these at each seeing. If the first method is pursued, the aspects successively apprehended will be related to one another to form an appraisal of the film as a whole; like a crystal built up facet by facet, whose interior construction is appreciated before its wholeness is revealed. This whole or unity is in the film the determinant of the multitude of variables which the director controls, and without which the unity would not exist; and whereas it is the last stage to be reached by the first method, it is the starting point of the second. In this case, the film as a whole, which is enriched with every extra seeing up to the point of equilibrium, resembles a fully grown crystal under a microscope, which reveals a different set of facets when regarded from each possible aspect, and yet retains unbroken the wholeness which would enable it to be seen altogether by a ubiquitous eye, just as the work of art can be grasped altogether even by the finite mind.

A special case of the second method of appreciation is uniquely the best when a film can only be seen once, and probably the best when it can only be seen a less than optimum number of times. Here it will be advisable to press forward attention and assimilation along every line until the return to them is equal at the margin. The reason for this procedure is easily seen. It depends on two assumptions: first, that the powers of receptivity of the spectator are limited; this is evidently true, since otherwise there would be no difficulty in understanding every aspect of a film at a single seeing. Second, that successive doses of attention to a single factor will be diminishingly rewarded; this also on reflection will be acknowledged true. If, then, the equi-marginal condition is not fulfilled, it will be profitable to transfer some of the attention from factors which are being rewarded with less to those which are meeting with more satisfaction at the margin. This process will be continued until no further substitution brings about any increase of satisfaction; and at this point rewards at the margin will be equal.

This only expresses in concise and accurate terms a fact which is widely recognized. Thus, the average filmgoer often remarks that, if he were as 'critical' as his more observant friend, he would not extract nearly as much enjoyment from films as he obtains by primitive and simple appreciation. It is indeed true that if he tried to discover the margins of a back-projected scene or the methods of moving the camera, he would fuss his mind and gain no enjoyment from it, but would lose much by letting slip the story through division of attention. It may well be, however, that the friend's knowledge of films is far more searching, so that all his margins, including the story and the stars, are farther advanced than the other man's.

The limit of concentration demanded by a film or play must be set lower than that demanded by a novel, a poem or a piece of music (now that gramophone records are readily available). This is because a film cannot conveniently and inexpensively be seen more than once (or at the most twice); whereas a difficult passage in a poem can be re-read as often as is necessary to master it. The difference is, of course, only of degree; but at present, when so many of the best films are banned or withheld from exhibition for commercial reasons, their true value is impossible to appreciate. Thus, until greater facilities are provided for the re-seeing of films, their development must proceed extensively as much as intensively; that is to say, their intelligence should be increased until the degree of attention now demanded by the few best sequences has to be maintained throughout the film. The commercial cinema, however, has nothing to fear from the danger of over-concentration of treatment. Its products may be appreciated with the utmost ease; and even at the first seeing it is possible to speculate profitably on matters of studio mechanism, which in any true work of art would be set aside for more important aspects, until an opportunity occurred for seeing the film again.

25. Having completed our study of technique, we can turn to discuss the relation which it bears to subject-matter. Aesthetic theories are as a rule divided according to the nature they assign to the value of art; here we shall simply distinguish those which hold that the work of art[1] is itself valuable, and that subject-matter is necessary but indifferent, from those which make subject the determining factor and appraise works of art by the effect which

[1] Reference may be made, in view of the prevailing confusion, to the way in which the terms 'art' and 'beauty' are here used. Art, as contrasted with beauty, is by definition valuable. Beauty is a unique and unanalysable quality common to those things which we call beautiful; it is thus not reducible to the useful, the agreeable or the morally good. Beauty is a necessary, though sometimes a non-valuable, constituent of art.

they produce on the spectator. The first kind of theory we shall call Deontological; it includes the schools of Kant, Coleridge and Croce: the second Teleological, those of Plato, Tolstoy and Marx. Properly stated, neither of these two categories of theory is self-contradictory, nor are they compatible or reducible to one another. Hence a protagonist of one cannot be persuaded by argument to exchange it for the other; he can only be led to understand more clearly what he previously believed in a confused way, while any minor inconsistencies in his attitude can be brought into the open and so rejected.

26. Before discussing the implications of these theories a difficulty must be removed. Art and natural beauty are commonly held to be co-extensive with the experience of beauty as a whole; and it is beauty, in virtue of its status as an ultimate value, which has been held in the past to lend value to art. Marxists, however, while admitting that beauty is an essential quality of art, hold that it makes no contribution to its value; and it might thus seem that the terms 'art', 'artist' and 'work of art', inseparably bound up as they are to us with associations of the value of beauty, would be improperly applied to productions of the Marxist school. But, as these terms are indispensable to the exposition of aesthetics, they are here retained with the looser connotation which

enables them to cover the extremest theories discussed.

Teleological theories are divided into two main branches, the moral and the social. The moral theory, which in recent times has been most uncompromisingly supported by Tolstoy, was discredited for a long time after his death by the crudeness with which he had stated it; but of late years it has been revived, notably by T. S. Eliot, in much more philosophical and coherent form. As a plea for the reconstitution of a living tradition to be maintained by orthodoxy, it has made a strong appeal to a generation wearying of continual change, of heresy for heresy's sake.[1] But, important as this movement is, it is outside the province of this book. The only morality known to the cinema, fear of the censor, is nothing better than expedience. It is there to the Social Teleologists, and in this class to the Marxists, that we must look for a consistent teleological ideal of art. Marxists affirm that the sole function of the artist is to focus some desirable aspect of social life on the members of a group or a community, in order to convince them of its rightness and awake them to the necessity of realizing it in practice. In this way the artist is closely aligned to the position of other citizens; *their* function is to undertake social tasks of

[1]For the precise connotation of these words, see Mr. Eliot's *After Strange Gods*.

whose importance they have been persuaded; *he*, by his aptitude in manipulating the instruments which have a power over the hearts and minds of men, is intrusted with the direction of their activity into the right channels. The artist therefore has two main tasks preparatory to his undertaking a work of art: to study, first, the objects and methods of the society he lives in, and, second, the qualities and failings of its members. In this way he identifies himself as profoundly as he can with the society (or, if he is a revolutionary, opposes it as vigorously as he can); and is thus able, by the later process, to exert on it the most general and permanent influence. Only a subsidiary importance, therefore, is attached to the artist's regard for his technique. Technique is bound up with subject-matter; and bound up not merely in the sense that there can be no technique without subject, but that, in addition, the subject is to govern the technique. It results from this that the artist does not, as in an individualistic state, select his subject for its adaptability to his medium; he finds it ready to hand in the forms of social persuasion which the state at any moment demands. And as society departs more and more from the simplicity of structure in which the importance of the individual predominates, and tends towards a complex interplay of almost mechanical parts, Marxist art deserts personal for social themes; it gains in intellect what it loses in emotion; it cross-sections society instead of typifying it; and becomes a text-book rather than an aesthetic experience. There is no place to-day, according to the Marxist, for a Milton or Shakespeare to embody with outstanding genius in single characters the qualities of a whole religion or of an extensive class in society. The single individual, Satan, Odysseus, Macbeth, however fully and finely conceived, cannot do justice to the minute differentiation of talent and character to subdivided function which the modern proletarian state can accomplish. What is required is an artist who can see society in terms of the facets of organizations and institutions which, abutting on one another at different angles, compose layer by layer the body of the social structure. In this respect the cinema is the ideal weapon of Marxist art. Proceeding by the method of conflict and sharp distinction of these facets, it reveals the dialectical composition of the state, at the lowest level working on the most primitive characteristics of the mob by means of the physiological clashes first generated by Eisenstein, and afterwards through the mechanism of obliquity impressing on the developed intellect the subtler shades of division and combination which a highly organized society employs. Everywhere the processes of conflict and reconciliation are at work; and the cinema, which as an artistic medium is bound to represent growth in terms of conflict, as a social instrument is therefore perfectly adapted to the Marxist ideal.

If artistic genius be a mere intensification of these talents, the best Marxist artist must be a genius; but if, in the common usage of the term, he is a man of exceptional sensibility in his awareness of beauty and his understanding of the emotions of his fellow men, the Marxist has little use for him. He must aspire instead to a mastery of sociology, politics and economics; acquire the ability to use the tools of his medium without effort; and be more concerned to say things than to be saying them. It will now be clear that the most vehement opponent of this theory should not deny the term 'art' to its best productions. It is true that they ignore beauty and the expression of emotion; but, on the other hand, they attain a unity of structure and wholeness of statement which have always hitherto been considered necessary but not sufficient conditions of the status of a work of art. Their insufficiency has been due to the stress hitherto laid on beauty, a quality whose effect is most noticeable in the private domains of life, and whose importance therefore dwindles before the Marxist ideal of a public community of living. As the sphere of private life is invaded by that of public life, the emotions peculiar to the former are to be replaced by the intellect communicable in the latter. Art will become the mechanism of persuasion and will be valued only as it issues in practical action. This action will be guided by intellect rather than emotion, by the forces which can be accurately communicated and foreseen rather than by those which are private, rebellious and difficult to assess.

27. The other main category of artistic theories, the Deontological, is also divided into a number of branches, according to the nature assigned to aesthetic experience. The two theories most widely held to-day are Expressionism and the theory of *Einfühlung*; but as the former, particularly in the modification developed by Mr. Carritt in *The Theory of Beauty*, is much the more plausible, it will alone be considered in what must perforce be a very brief sketch. Expressionism must not be confused with the view that art is dependent on communication. A melody or a landscape, if perfectly imagined in every detail, is not increased in artistic value by being embodied in a material medium. Yet such a public embodiment is as necessary in practice to the realization of a novel or a film (though not of an epigram) as it is to the construction of a theory of economics. But if communication is a practical, though not a theoretical, necessity to the production of works of art on a large scale, expression is the very nature of all art. 'That which has to be expressed and that which can express it first become beautiful when indis-

tinguishably fused in the expression. . . . A mountain, a poem, a song is beautiful to the man whose feelings are expressed in it; and it makes no difference whether we say that it expresses them to him or he expresses them in it. . . . The writer of a poem expresses his passion in it. It expresses the passion to me, but only on condition that I have some such passion to express. The truth is that in reading a poem I express myself in it, I find words for what I have already been, and so first come fully to know it.'[1] 'The great artists reveal us to ourselves because their imagination is identical with our own, and the difference between us is merely one of degree.'[2] It is thus in the expression of emotion that the aesthetic value of words, colours and sounds resides. If they impart historical or philosophical truths as well, that will affect their status as history or philosophy, but it will be irrelevant to their value as art. Art, then, or any experience of beauty, reigns solely in the imagination and does not pronounce on the reality of its objects; it is, therefore, a theoretical rather than a practical activity, so that, in the words of Kant: '*Taste* is the faculty of judging of an object or a method of representing it by an *entirely disinter-*

[1] Carritt, *op. cit.* p. 182.
[2] *Ib.* 195. In these passages Mr. Carritt is stating Croce's theory, which appears, however, to coincide here with his own.

ested satisfaction or dissatisfaction. The object of such satisfaction is called *beautiful*.'[1] 'That of which we are aware, then, is not thereby beautiful; it only becomes so when it is contemplated without practical interest, without scientific abstraction, and without existential judgment, *as* the pure expression of emotion.'[2] In the first part of this summary, Mr. Carritt denies Croce's identification of expression with intuition, which does not here concern us; in the second, he enumerates the features of the Expressionist theory which most sharply distinguish it from the Marxist.[3] To a first approximation, works which are pure art to one school are not art at all to the other. Thus, an inflammatory speech which stimulated but did not express emotion would be held to be art by a Marxist and denied that name by an Expressionist; while in the case of a fugue which did not provide even the most indirect incitement to action the position would be reversed. Works which are impure or mixed may be considered as art by both schools, but for different reasons. The Expressionist will approve them for the expression of an emotion which can be theoretically contemplated;

[1]*Critique of Judgement*, part i., div. 1, sec. 6. Bernard's translation.

[2]Carritt, *op. cit.* p. 288.

[3]Here, as before, used to typify teleological theories in general.

the Marxist for an urge to practical activity. These are not two elements existing side by side in works of art, but two ways of regarding the same elements. Nevertheless, though most actual works of art are mixed, and so may be appreciated by either school, the difference of emphasis we have noticed leads to a difference in the importance they attach to technique and to subject-matter. All subjects are equally suited to the Expressionist, for all are equally capable of confused and clear expression. But to the Marxist subjects are graduated in importance according to the current scale of social necessity. And though it might happen that the Expressionist chose a subject high in the Marxist scale of values, this would be unlikely; for the claims of contemplation and stimulation conflict; and though a low degree of both may co-exist, a high degree of one indicates an almost complete absence of the other.

28. This divergence in the choice of subject is reproduced in the importance attached to technique. To the Expressionist, the chief criterion of value is the degree of clearness of expression of a particular emotion attained in a given work of art. The artist cannot even feel the emotion clearly and fully without translating it by technique, even if only in his mind, into the form of one or other of the arts. Technique, therefore, even in the first and innermost process of creation, is essential to art and a

271

prime object of the artist's study; for it will largely determine at what point in the scale his art will lie between the crude matter of emotion and its controlled and contemplated expression. And the appreciator, whose art on this theory must be the same in kind, though it may be different in degree, from the artist's, is in the same position; for he cannot express his feelings through, let us say, a film, unless he has been accustomed to this process by formulating films in his mind; and if his knowledge of technique is defective, his expression will be correspondingly confused and inadequate. Nor can this theory be held to lend colour to the pretensions of virtuosity. Degrees of beauty can only be produced by degrees of extension and subtlety of expression (so that a film may be greater than one of its sequences), by degrees of expressiveness of the same feeling (so that Constable's several drafts of *The Leaping Horse* may be ranged in value), and by degrees of depth, in which a less or greater number of elements intransigent to expression are fused into a successful work of art.[1] None of these criteria give a high place to virtuosity, which is the abandonment of expression as the aim of art, and the substitution of technical dexterity.

The artist's development, therefore, proceeds along the parallel lines of imagination and technique, these being of equal importance and inseparable in

[1] Carritt, *op. cit.* pp. 214-218.

the work of art. Technique is not a means to expression, nor expression a mere excuse for employing technique. But this is very different from the Marxist attitude. Here the artist's sole aim is the advancement of society, though this no doubt is accompanied by its proper pleasure, just as is virtue, knowledge or beauty. There is usually no claim upon him to perfect his technique, since the power of influencing others to action is seldom directly coordinated with clarity of expression. But even where the text-book ideal has prevailed, and concepts have to be accurately conveyed, the importance of technique must be disregarded, or at least never stressed. The desire to rid the mind of incoherent feeling in the calm contemplation of artistic expression is apparently deep-seated; and it is encouraged by a sense of the value of technique. The Marxist, therefore, to whom expression for its own sake is anathema, must transfer attention from technique to subject, distracting it from what is important as a means but undesirable as an end, and concentrating it on what is at a farther remove itself only a means, for the art whose importance lies in its subject-matter is only important in conducing to the intellectual and social advancement of the state.

In Expressionist and Marxist art, therefore, both subject and technique are necessary: but to the one the former is irrelevant in judgments of value, to the other the latter. In either case there is justification for the abstraction of technique from subject on which the structure of this and the last chapter is based. In the case of Expressionism, this is obvious; in that of Marxism, there must be a practical excuse. The subject-matter on which it is desirable to concentrate may be indicated in extent, but is too vast to particularize; the technique on which it is undesirable to concentrate may be completely surveyed, and fairly deeply, though of course less fully, analysed. The Marxist reader must on these grounds excuse an inversion of the space he would choose to allot to these two parts of the subject; the Expressionist will be glad of the convenient coincidence between the structure of art as he sees it and the exigencies of exposition.

Chapter VII

Categories of the Film: *b.* Descriptions

'It is for the heart to suggest our problems; it is for the intellect to solve them. . . . The position for which the intellect is primarily adapted is to be the servant of the social sympathies.'

COMTE

1. *Origin of the documentary movement in the class struggle.* 2. *The film symphony and the documentary movement.* 3. *Definition of the documentary: Mr. Grierson;* 4. *Mr. Braun;* 5. *Mr. Blakeston.* 6. *A new definition suggested and tested by several criteria.* 7. *Characteristics of the documentary.* 8. *The danger of categories in making films: their necessity in criticizing them.* 9. *The imagist film.* 10. *The synthetic film: description by degrees of naturalism;* 11. *the silhouette film;* 12. *the model film;* 13. *the drawn film.* 14. *The limitations of the synthetic film in respect of unrealism.* 15. *Conclusions.*

1.   All but a very few of the films which are 'featured' in English cinemas conform to a single type. Their stories have proved successful on the stage, and have been associated with the names of well-known actors; transferred to the screen, their

casts may have changed, but it is certain that their mode of presentation will remain the same. The three or four scenes of the original play will have been extended to twenty or thirty (all indoors, as a rule); and within each of these sets several camera positions will be provided. The acting will be theatrical acting, modified by the demands of lights and microphones; the dialogue will have been adapted from the play, and often in English films toned down a little, so as to preclude any chance of misunderstanding or make any calls on a lethargic audience. Often the camera will roam round the set in aimless pursuit of the characters, as if to demonstrate, were this necessary, the solid and expensive nature of the furnishings, and the technical resources of the studio. The transferences from shot to shot will be enfeebled by every device from the laboratories by which the audience can be lulled into sleep. When the dialogue is more than usually inadequate to the emotional needs of the story, a faint saccharine sound, a syrup of music, will well up from behind, sometimes prolonging an estrangement which a moment's good sense would have reconciled, sometimes mercifully heralding the happy ending of the film.

In an attempt to break away from this world of platitude and artifice, the documentary movement was founded. The U.S.S.R. had long recognized that the cinema could stir the minds of the people, making real to them the countless activities which contributed to their well-being, even though they might never see the majority of those who cooperated with them in the life of the state. Thus was born a sense of the hardships which were suffered by many of the less fortunate; and a feeling that they could be shared through the special efforts of the rest. This was particularly necessary in a new society which, in the face of the productive efficiency of modern machinery and organization, had to forgo great possible improvements in the standards of life, for the sake of a faster accumulation of capital instruments.

In capitalist countries a similar change of attitude occurred. It was felt that the quiet, cultivated life of the last two centuries, in which the ideals of the connoisseur and even the dilettante had been highly praised, must give place to a life of struggle. The rise to power and education of the proletariat had intensified the competition for work, and had at first evoked the sympathy and help of the upper classes, by waking them to the abuses to which unrestrained capitalism had subjected the propertyless poor. The contest for power strained the existing social and political machinery, so that none knew whether it could be mended in its original form, or must be totally recast. Those who were, or imagined themselves to be, precluded from responsibility in the state taunted the rich with their idleness and preoccupation with pleasure; the rich in part rebutted the charge by renouncing much of their previous luxury, as they had to do, in order to meet the higher wages which unionism had forced out of them, and the declining profits which resulted from years of continuing depression.

The arts had a difficult time in the conflict, tending sometimes to be submerged, sometimes exalted as instruments of propaganda. The spread of education and the slow equalization of wealth should have given a great impetus to a better and wider appreciation of art. Some improvement was indeed noticeable, as is evidenced in England by the success of the promenade concerts and the special exhibitions at Burlington House; but two contrary influences prevented it from being very marked. In the first place, art, which, as we have said, bore the stigma of idleness, was cleverly rendered respectable by being transmuted into entertainment. Anything which made money and provided pleasure for the masses was doubly justified; it added to the national wealth and gave happiness to those who lacked it most. Standards did not matter much; even hedonism is better than misery. On the other hand, those who really believed in the necessity of art were half-ashamed of their faith; they decried 'art for art's

278

sake', and the escape into dreams and savage civilizations in which the post-war Romantics had indulged. Obsessed with the conditions of modern men, especially working men, in an industrial community, they thought that the sole justification of art lay in its ability to criticize the social structure, or inform the community of ills which it must remedy and ideals to which as representative of the state it must aspire. The individual and his near surroundings were no longer considered the microcosm of society; the poetry of the self gave way to the poetry of the mass.

.These are the tendencies to be remarked in the English documentary cinema of to-day. They are best expressed by Mr. Grierson, who declares: 'Theory of naturals apart, it [*sc.* Flaherty's philosophy] represents an escapeism (a wan and distant eye) which tends in lesser hands to sentimentalism. . . . Indeed you may feel that in individualism[1] is a yahoo tradition largely responsible for our present anarchy, and deny at once both the hero of decent heroics (Flaherty) and the hero of indecent ones (studio). In this case you will feel vaguely that you want your drama in terms of some cross-section of reality which will reveal the essentially co-operative and mass nature of society; leaving the individual

[1]Apparently used here in the artistic, with no reference to the economic, use of the term.

to find his honours in the swoop of creative social forces. In other words you are liable to abandon the story form, and seek like the modern exponent of poetry painting and prose, a matter and method more satisfactory to the mind and spirit of the time.' That this is Mr. Grierson's own opinion is shown by the fact that the opposite view is never stated, while the next sentence continues as follows. 'Here begin the real theoretical troubles of documentary and the agony of financing it against the forces of romanticism.'[1] And again (suiting his style no doubt to the stress of which he is so acutely aware): 'Elton possibly unappreciative of radio's social significance and therefore lacking in proper (aesthetic) affection for subject. This point important, as affecting almost all the tyros of documentary. Too damned arty and post-war to get their noses into public issues.'[2]

2. It is this attitude which explains the objections of Mr. Grierson's school of thinking to the film symphony. Mr. Grierson himself writes: 'For this reason I hold the symphony tradition of cinema for a danger—and *Berlin* for the most dangerous of all film models to follow. There's dope in it. Unfortunately, the fashion is with such avoidance as *Berlin* represents. The highbrows bless the symphony for its good looks and, being sheltered rich little souls for

[1] *Cinema Quarterly*, vol. i. no. 2, pp. 70, 71-72.
[2] *Ib.* p. 118.

the most part, absolve it gladly from further inten-
tion. . . . They [sc. symphonic forms] present new
beauties and new shapes; they fail to present new
persuasions.'[1]

Some consideration must now be given to the
symphonic film, before a final return can be made
to the documentary in general, to discover what it
must include and what shut out. The symphony,[2]
like the abstract, is an attempt to generate aesthetic
emotion[3] through the film. Unlike the abstract,
material things may and often do form part of its
subject, but the feelings they normally arouse (love,
pity, fear and so on) play no part in the purpose of
the film, and should be suppressed. The symphony
is the apotheosis of form. By varying rhythms and
tempi, by massing and simplification, by interrela-
tion of the sound factor and the visual film, it attempts a correspondence with music and a divorce
from life. Thus, in its purest form, the symphony
becomes an abstract film; but, as we have said, natural objects gradually intrude themselves on the
director's mind; he selects them not wholly for their

[1]*Cinema Quarterly*, vol. i. no. 3, pp. 137-138.

[2]Used throughout as short for film symphony, and not for
musical symphony.

[3]Cf. Mr. Clive Bell's *Art* for the associations of this term.
Very roughly it means the unique emotion which pure art
produces, to which naturalistic representation, evoking the
normal emotions of life, is irrelevant.

formal, but in part for their 'story', value; and the result belongs to the type of *Berlin* or *Rien que les Heures*.

It will now be evident that the film symphony must be justified or condemned along with every other pure, or even non-social, work of art. It must not be distinguished on account of the greater expenditure it entails (which might be given to the poor); it is the cheapest type of film, often costing much less than the concert performance of a new piece of music, or the stage production of a new play.

Having removed this possible misconception, we may turn to examine the main issue. There can be no logical proof either way: the subject of discussion is a question of value, and can only be resolved by showing that there are implications of the realist standpoint which, once they are pointed out, conflict with the standards of value to which the realists themselves appeal. It is clear that in past periods of artistic activity, such as the age of Pericles or the Italian Renaissance, art, though widely appreciated by the people, was not used as a ventilator of social ills or a propagandist weapon of improvement. Even to-day, when the 'social conscience' is aroused as never before, the majority of artists, *qua* artists, are as little concerned with social and political problems as they were in the past. Among the poets, Eliot and Pound are concerned with the intricacies of the individual; no one could call them social ferments. But they, we are told, though heralds of the new poetic forms, are not representative of the new spirit. Auden, Spender and Lewis are certainly much concerned with the difficulties of relating the personal to the mass life; but it cannot be said that their poetry itself has a predominantly social value. In the first place, it is too difficult for the masses to master, and in the second, it is not directed outwards, as were the political lampoons of the eighteenth century, to capturing and converting the waverers. Music and painting are still more obviously removed from any attempt at persuasion; they present, indeed, new forms and beauties, but they demand acceptance for no creeds, whether old or new. In totalitarian states alone, where art is harnessed to political institutions, are Mr. Grierson's statements not only true, but tautologous. But, in affirming them of a democratic state such as our own, he runs contrary to the opinions of the modern poets, far more the modern composers and painters, of whom he would like to approve.

Having established a more reasonable attitude to the documentary film, we can revert to the matter of definition. Definition would not be so important if directors were content to make films as they were allowed to make them, instead of disputing about the class they fell into when made. But it is already plain that as much energy is spent in supporting the documentary film in general, by censuring its supposed competitors, as in making particular documentary films. When documentary directors are successful, they are thus doubly justified; when unsuccessful, they have at least the saving grace, denied to others, of having made such an exalted type of film.

3. Over the question of definition, which they are constantly attempting, the 'documentarians' are distressingly vague. The most succinct and widely quoted definition is that of Mr. Grierson. 'Documentary', he says, 'is the creative treatment of actuality'.[1] There is to be no limit to its practical powers. Mr. Rotha explains: 'Documentary defines not subject or style, but approach. It denies neither trained actors nor the advantages of staging. It justifies the use of every known technical artifice to gain its effect on the spectator. . . . To the documentary director the appearance of things and people is only superficial. It is the meaning behind the thing and the significance underlying the person that occupy his attention. . . . Documentary approach to cinema differs from that of story-film not in its disregard for craftsmanship, but in the purpose to which that craftsmanship is put. Documentary is a trade just as carpentry or pot-making.'[2] The pot-maker makes

[1] *Cinema Quarterly*, vol. 2, no. 1, p. 8.
[2] *Ib.* vol. 2, no. 2, p. 78.

pots, and the documentarian documentaries. We knew already what a pot was; we still know nothing of a documentary. Mr. Rotha thus jibs at actually stating what the approach is to be, and we fall back on Mr. Grierson's quoted definition. This, however, is as embracing as art itself. What artist could lay claim to the name if he were content with mechanical reproduction, and so abjured creation? What, then, can he do but 'treat', and what can he treat but actuality? And what certainty has Mr. Grierson in saying that some other artist's actuality is a mere appearance, a thing of trivial or transient significance? Everyone would no doubt agree that the average British and American film lacked creative interpretation. But even Mr. Grierson and his school would scarcely claim that, by a miraculous power of insight, they had discerned a monopoly of value in their own work. Any sincere and inspired film, therefore, whether it arose out of burning social indignation, conviction of the beneficent interrelations of industrial man, a desire to reveal the subconscious self, or the fantastic dreams of an opium-eater, would be classed as documentary. This is misplaced catholicity, confusing descriptive classifications with normative standards of excellence. A clearer definition must be sought elsewhere.

4. It is no more to be found among the symphonists than among the documentarians. Thus Mr.

Braun writes in an editorial article in *film art* entitled *film: definition*[1]: 'The real film is the visual poem.

'The real film is the representation of incidents and emotions by moving masses of light variations.

'It is the expression *through cinematic form*[2] of the matters or emotions to be expressed. . . . *Film is not a representation of reality.*'[2]

He goes on to affirm that the story is by no means excluded from the true film, and that the abstract is a means of exciting emotion. Setting aside the resounding tautology (the form of the cinema is cinematic), we find that the definition is quite as wide as Mr. Grierson's. It does indeed exclude sound (without giving any reasons), but it includes the film symphony, the personal film and the documentary, as distinguished and defined below.[3] All these are intended to portray incidents and emotions: they could hardly escape the former if they wished to do so, while the latter is only less inevitable if 'emotions' are supposed to mean 'good emotions'. In that event, the definition begs the question, by not saying what 'good' or 'desirable' is meant to include; just as cinematic, as quoted above, meant no more than cinema without further explanation, and was thus

[1]Winter 1933. Mr. Braun is an erratic adherent of the miniscular movement.
[2]Original italicized.   [3]pp. 290-295.

tautologous. What is excluded is the sound film of any type; the abstract film, as defined above[1]; and the lecture film. Mr. Braun thus defines the cinema; but documentary is nowhere mentioned or defined; nothing is heard of it, despite its evident importance, and the inclusive title of Mr. Braun's leading article.

5. Another attempt, however, has been made—this time to identify the documentary with the lecture film. The lecture film isolates a group of phenomena; speeds, slows or magnifies them to make them clearer; describes in words relations and purposes which cannot be seen; but otherwise remains neutral. It is descriptive, rather than normative; it comments, but does not correct. This, according to one school of thought, is the only sphere of documentary. In a *Manifesto on the Documentary Film*, Mr. Blakeston says: 'Years ago the documentary film had value because it presented us with facts: from the documents of four or five years ago it was possible to learn.' He then goes on, with scarcely veiled reference to the work of Wright and Elton, to denounce the modern documentary, and concludes: 'To repeat: we are incensed because films are shown to the public, who are always about five years behind and have just dimly associated "document" with "culture", under false prestige and false pretences:

[1]p. 281. See also p. 293 below.

were these films to be presented to the public as drama, the exhibitors would be lynched.

'To repeat: we want documents which will show, with the clarity and logic of a scholar's thesis, the subjects they are supposed to tackle; we want no more filtered skies, "Russian" montage and other vulgarities in our "educational" productions.'[1]

This is a fair example of the controversies to which confused definition and the misrepresentation of motives give rise. The G.P.O. films were never meant to fulfil the purpose for the non-fulfilment of which Mr. Blakeston criticizes them so harshly; and, on the other hand, the documentary as he defines it is still flourishing and in no need of angry protest, as the *Secrets of Nature* series makes plain.

It has been necessary to introduce this subject at some length, in order to achieve three purposes: first, to expose by quotation from accepted sources the muddle and recrimination to which the documentary film has given rise; second, to explain the influences which have brought the realistic school into being, and so to excuse what at any other time would have been considered its excesses; but thirdly, to appeal for a more charitable approach to the romantic film, which is likely to be, if less urgent in the present, at least more important in the future.

6. Having thus cleared the ground and arrayed the

[1]*Close-Up*, Dec. 1933.

necessary material, it is possible to proceed to the constructive task of definition, and complete it fairly quickly. It will already be clear that definition is better based on material and technique (which are comparatively public) than on attitude and motive (which are conducive to quarrels and misinterpretations). We shall therefore try to approach the subject in an abstract and impartial manner, so that everyone can agree what documentary *is*, even though all do not agree that it is good. The top line of the chart shows a scale extending from exact reproduction at the one extreme to non-reproduction, or 'haphazardness', at the other. All films (and indeed all works of art) contain elements which are to be found at different points on this scale; and we propose to define documentary as a span which we shall try to indicate as clearly as possible. The definition is as follows. 'The documentary film is in subject and approach a dramatized presentation of man's relation to his institutional life, whether industrial, social or political; and in technique, a subordination of form to content.' The criteria which such a definition should satisfy are the following. (1) inclusion of a well-marked group of films, to which at least some people at present apply the word defined; (2) exclusion of other groups, to which other names can be given; (3) ease of classification of films in the defined groups; (4) absence of overlapping and unimportance of marginal cases. We shall now apply these criteria to the proposed definition.

(1) The most widely separated type of film which Mr. Grierson's school call documentary are his own and Flaherty's. Grierson's films deal with modern industrial life in the framework of its institutions, emphasizing the relation of man to institution, rather than of man to man. They are thus amply covered; but so also are Flaherty's films. These, indeed, commonly portray a primitive civilization, in which it might be thought that institutions played an unimportant part. But this is by no means the case. Modern civilization, where democratic, has tended to frame its institutions in such a way that the lives they regulate are freed for their most important tasks. The facilities of education, defence, health and unemployment insurance, and the mechanisms of improved transport and communication, relieve men from the drudgery of life, so that they may cultivate art, science and personal relations. This ideal is at present fulfilled with extreme imperfection; but in this sense, with each improvement, the relation of men to their institutions will become not closer, but more remote.

A savage community, however, is quite otherwise. Physically, it is on the brink of life; spiritually, on the brink of the supernatural. Where the conditions are so stringent, the institutions will be stringent also. The individual must obey without question, and regulate his every action by tribal laws. His community, like the totalitarian state, owes its existence to its efficiency; freedom is the reward of security, paid for by forfeit of much material advantage. Hence, primitive man exists largely in relation to his institutions; a film of his life is well covered by our use of the term documentary.

(2) We saw how Mr. Grierson's definition merely excluded bad films, even if interpreted charitably. Ours, however, if treated in the same manner, is much narrower. Let us consider:

(i) The lecture film, which may very well deal with institutions, and is certain, as we have said, to subordinate form to content. On the other hand, its material is selected in such a way as to reveal hidden relations, and present vividly in pictures what the text-book relies on an occasional diagram to explain; drama, if present at all, is irrelevant. Dramatization, however, is the chief aim of the documentary, and the chief characteristic of drama is conflict. If the subject of the documentary is to be human institutions, it must represent the conflicts between man and his fellows, and between man and nature, which compelled him to erect this framework of institutions to live in. Drama necessitates conflict; conflict and its resolution is the motive of institutional life. Hence the lecture film and the documentary

291

are sharply distinguished, even when their subject and technique are similar; for the one impartially records while the other intensifies the struggle, simplifying the issues in order to present them more dramatically. The tissue of necessary forms and conventions which the lecture film explains and relates, it is the business of documentary to tear aside, revealing the forces of order and disorder, the harmonies and conflicts, which are ever at work below. In this way the documentary passes over into the propaganda film. All men who are sufficiently interested to inquire will agree on the forms and mechanisms of government; but may well differ over the motive which inspires their working, the benefits they confer, and the need for their continuance or destruction. It is thus that impartiality in this field is difficult, though not perhaps impossible to achieve. All degrees of bias must be admitted to the documentary film, if only because they are so hard to assess. A representation of the working population as labouring under unjust hardships which national ownership would soon correct would be regarded by most socialists as a mild statement, but by most capitalists as a gross travesty of the facts.[1]

[1]Mr. N. L. Spottiswoode, on the other hand, excludes propaganda from the documentary film (see *film*, spring 1933). His distinction, however, seems to rest on an inadequate appreciation of the relativity of the truth of social judgments.

(ii) The personal film. This term is suggested, not as being wholly satisfactory, but as an improvement on the usual 'story film'. It refers to the films whose main interest is focused on human relations which, though conditioned by their social environment, have an importance which transcends it. Thus, in subject they fall into the category of Shakespeare's plays and the Greek tragedies. They are dramatic, and they as a rule subordinate form to content; but they are not primarily concerned with institutions, and so are not documentary films.

(iii) The film symphony. This, we have said, may have institutions as its subject, and be dramatic in its form. In technique, however, it deals with pure components which produce aesthetic emotion, and its subject is only of importance in contributing to this. Masses, velocities, light-values and tempi may be derived from shots of factories or men at work; but these have no institutional significance in the film.

(iv) Lastly, there is the abstract, or 'absolute', film, whose ideals are those of the symphony, but whose material bears no resemblance whatever to objects as they occur in nature. This type also is excluded in the definition. It subordinates subject to form, and takes no stock of institutions.

Nevertheless, his article shows a much more acute insight into the problem than is common in discussions of it.

(3) Classification will be considered by giving a few instances of well-known films of varied merit, which carry with them in the mind associations with a large group having intentions similar to the film mentioned. (i) The *Secrets of Nature* series. Dr. Canti's medical films. (ii) Disney's cartoons. *The Private Life of Henry VIII. The Conquerors. Extase.* (iii) *Berlin. La Marche des Machines.* The abstract sequences in *Metropolis.* (iv) The Fischingers' musical abstracts. Lye's colour abstract. The documentary, which is of course residual to this classification, would include *Contact, Moana, Industrial Britain, Aero-engine.*

(4) The problem of marginal cases will prove troublesome to any definition which does not include every film that could possibly be made. Some of the Russian films do not fit very conveniently into the classification we have given. Thus *October* and *Deserter* are evidently documentary. But *Earth* is almost equally concerned with pure form (*e.g.* the opening and closing sequences of the apples in the rain; and the compositions of men and beasts against the sky); and with the attitude of the poet to the cycle of birth, growth, decay and death; and with the sociological conflicts of the *kulaki* and the collectives. It is thus by turns a film symphony, a personal film and a documentary, and cannot be relegated to any one class. Again, Cavalcanti's *Rien que les Heures*

has the rhythms, albeit somewhat tentative, of the pure film; but it has also the prostitutes, hags on the verge of suicide, and dismal streets, which are the usual apparatus of the social reformer and the documentary. These, however, provide no reason for rejecting the definition, until it can be shown that they are avoided by some alternative which suffers no comparative disadvantage in other respects.

7. A final word may be said of the characteristics of the documentary, which is now at length defined. Its purpose, as conceived by Mr. Grierson and his group, is that associated with the Soviet cinema. It is less a text-book than a tract; it makes ordinary people conscious of the life and work of the state, showing the empire in particular as a system of co-operation rather than compulsion. To this end, it does not attempt to explain in minute detail the processes it treats of; rather it enforces on the spectators their place in the social structure, the good or ill which they do. To this end also it dramatizes the relation between man and machine; or contrasts the emptiness of life before the coming of an invention with the education or delight which it brings.

To this conception there are certain corollaries of technique. Natural types are used in preference to actors; they are the men who are accustomed to particular pieces of work, which they continue to do before the camera exactly as they had always done.

They are not called upon to display any subtlety of expression or grace of movement which is not inherent in their task. In an exceptional case these qualities might be absent, and yet wanted; there would then be no bar to the use of trained actors. On the side of the camera, there is scope for every device of angle and speed which makes the presentation of a scene more forcible. There is, of course, a danger that the mere tricks and affectations may be introduced of which Mr. Blakeston bitterly complains; but his own documentary is only safer from criticism because, attempting so much less, it is so much less easy to fail. Cutting and camera are both exploited to the utmost: Mr. Rotha, in a brilliant drop-hammer sequence in *Roadwards*, brings the spectator into the closest touch with the machinery, so that he *feels* its force intensely, but only understands its working in the vaguest manner. On the other hand, methods of exposition must be subordinated to the main sociological theme. That theme must be chosen for its importance, not for its adaptability to the screen.

8. What has been said above in criticism of the definition of documentary implies not the smallest criticism of the documentary directors themselves. Films are justified not by fitting into categorical boxes, but by springing from sincerity, purpose and knowledge. It is only the literary task of criticism

which necessitates accurate classification, to assist the handling of concepts by which the understanding of films is ultimately furthered.

9. We turn now to the imagist film, which is an attempt to use the visual simile and the symbol as the chief means of montage, and as an alternative to the spoken word. The symbol will here be differentiated from the simile by applying the term to indirect[1] suggestions which are inherent in the material of the film, instead of being drawn in from without. Thus in *Extase* (Machaty, 1933)[2] a coming storm was indicated by shots of statues of horses, leaping forward with their manes flying in the wind (this was a simile); and in the same film, the mating horses, bees and waving corn, which took part in the surroundings of the characters in the Carpathian mountains, were symbols for the ecstatic love which the woman in the film had lately found. The visual simile has already been discussed at length, and no more need be said of it here. The symbol has the advantage over it of being integral with the action, instead of an interruption of its continuity; but it

[1]This word, of course, evades the basic issues of symbol and simile alike; but it allows a distinction to be drawn at a superficial level of inquiry proper to a minor issue in the present book.

[2]Not publicly exhibited in England because, being unequivocally frank instead of prurient, it was considered indecent and suggestive.

has the disadvantage of being very rarely applicable. The cinema, indeed, can select and magnify any detail of symbolic value in a scene; but even then the scope of symbolism is likely to be restricted, unless its language is to become far-fetched or esoteric. *Extase* was by far the finest imagist film yet made, and was aided by a story of great simplicity; and yet in many places it became obscure, and merely seemed to suggest a meaning which could not be clearly grasped. But this was a fault which re-seeing removed; and the symbol, when carefully chosen, having many layers of meaning which the thoughtful mind can in turn strip off, is able to give a depth to the cinema which its warmest advocates must admit to have been hitherto absent. The imagist film, using plain naturalism with every device of montage in the simpler passages, symbolism when it is available without straining, and the visual simile to convey more complicated concepts, is the most powerful silent film. It cannot well be combined with speech, which in large quantities will upset its construction, and in small quantities will refuse to amalgamate with the visual film, if music is already playing an important part;[1] but music alternated with and arising out of natural sound should be amply sufficient to complete the comparatively simple explanations demanded by the subjects

[1] See p. 192 above.

best fitted to the cinema on other grounds. If true films can never be subtle, they will ultimately be profound as well as simple.

10. The film, as we have hitherto described it, places considerable reliance on the forms and arrangements which are found in the natural world. It is true that a number of differentiating factors enable distortions, patterns and purposes to be stamped on the natural material of each shot; while a number of types of montage extend these modifications to the whole film which is compounded from these shots. Nevertheless, though the natural film diverges far from nature, the synthetic film diverges at least as far from the natural film. We have already, in Chapter II, described how the synthetic film may be divided according to the degree of this divergence. At one extreme, the abstract film approaches no closer to natural arrangement than the elements of paper or wire, gathered from places far apart, which compose it. Next, the cartoons of the Hungarian artist Zuts, though they represent living forms of animals and trees, are drawn with a non-natural economy of line, and frequently unravel and resolve themselves into abstract patterns. The early cartoons of Walt Disney travel a little further towards representation. Their figures are recognizably natural, and remain so; but they undergo extraordinary transformations, and perform evolutions in

299

defiance of the laws of nature. They are protean, but not abstract. Disney's later cartoons move still closer to the natural film, though they do not nearly reach it. In *The Pied Piper*, for instance, there are : transformations of a violent kind, so that the piper's magic is rendered doubly effective by contrasting with the naturalness of Hamlin. There now appear films of a hybrid type like *King Kong*, in which the synthetic element, here a gigantic ape, is supposed to reach the level of naturalness of the rest of the film. On the other hand, a few natural films (e.g. *The Cabinet of Dr. Caligari*) synthesize their settings to such a degree that they become almost synthetic films. The human form is intractable, but can be modified by optical distortion. Thus the scale is complete from one extreme to the other.

11. This classification, though most suitable for a theoretical study, cannot well be applied to actual instances of synthetic films. For the partially empirical treatment used here, a division according to material is to be preferred; and we shall pass over the abstract film, to which sufficient reference has been made. The next most tenuous synthetic type is the *silhouette film*, for whose development Lotte Reiniger is alone responsible. Her figures are black on a light background, and move solely in the plane of the screen. It would seem to be easy to track the camera up to them, if necessary; but in fact this is not done.

The effect of naturalness produced is very much restricted. The figures can pass one another, but cannot advance or recede into the distance. Their movements also are a little stiff and jerky, and their appearance is one of complete flatness. The subjects suited to the silhouette film are delicate and fragile romances. There is no hope of engaging the emotions of the spectator, who can but regard the action as he would a puppet-show. Mme. Reiniger is, of course, well aware of these limitations, as is shown by *Carmen, Harlekin, The Flying Coffer, Dr. Dolittle's Adventures,* etc. The sound factor presents certain difficulties. Parts of *Ten Minutes with Mozart* were synchronized with human singing voices. The fullness and body of these voices shattered the figures in the attempt at amalgamation. If speech were required to explain the action, a high squeaky voice might be used, as was done to represent the Gnat in the broadcast version of *Alice.* Musically, the most satisfactory accompaniment has proved to be an arrangement of early chamber music, which largely contributed to the superiority of *Harlekin* over the other silhouette films.

12. At the opposite extreme of substantiality is the model film. It suffers, however, from the same remoteness from life, perhaps because of the jerkiness of movement imposed by the difficulty of advancing solid figures through very small distances.

The most ambitious model film, *The Mascot* (Stare-witch, 1933), in which toy animals moved about among the feet of human beings, was broken up by heterogeneity; animals and humans existed in different worlds; and the attempt which the film made to relate them was rendered futile from the start. This difficulty cannot be overcome until models can be given the fluidity which is inseparable from almost all movements in the natural world. The same fault was to be found in *King Kong*, a film about the adventures of a mythical ape, which was discovered along with other prehistoric creatures on a remote island visited by a film-producing company. The monsters were not so much Pleistocene as plasticine; they met the film stars in battle across a gulf as wide as that which separates the lions in Trafalgar Square from the diminutive pedestrians who pass them by. Not until the technical capabilities of the cinema are far advanced will the synthetic films discussed up to this point have any great artistic value.

13. It is otherwise, however, with the entirely flat, drawn film, best exemplified in the work of Walt Disney. Fluidity of movement he achieved long ago; and more recently he has added the subjective application of colour.[1] It is only when some degree of naturalism has been attained that such departures from naturalism have any value. If Disney's crea-

[1]See p. 152 above.

tures leap from buildings and remain sitting in the air, we are only surprised and entertained because we had supposed them to be subject to the laws of gravitation. Kong, sitting on top of the Empire State Building, was no more likely to fall than an isosceles triangle. The synthetic film, a term which we shall now reserve to the class here under discussion, surmounts these obstacles with ease, and prompts an inquiry into more difficult problems. If the synthetic film suffered no disabilities in comparison with the natural film, it would be a more valuable medium; for it could approach as close to nature, or depart as far from it, as the artist at any time required. We have already seen how colour can be controlled over a range inconceivable to the photographer of nature; composition may be simplified, stylized or adorned; and movements of flight, which were hitherto confined to the theatre of the imagination, can now be embodied on the screen.

14. The synthetic film, however, is now subject to a heavy limitation: it must be our business to see whether this can ultimately be removed. We saw in Chapter III that there was a part of personality which films by their very nature could not convey. But there is another transmissible part, upon which depends the contact with humanity essential to the vitality of the cinema. It has not proved itself a good pure medium, like music; only in the representation

of life has it an opportunity to excel. It must therefore be capable of arousing emotions, and it cannot do this unless its spectators are convinced of the 'aliveness' of characters upon the screen. From written descriptions we are accustomed to construct figures which are as emotionally potent as human beings in the flesh, though they originated in mere marks on paper. But in a pictorial medium some degree of representation is necessary. In fantastic comedy, it need be very slight. Incongruity is the basis of humour; but did it not diverge from a recognizable humanity, it would not be truly incongruous at all. Disagreement implies a common ground. In more serious branches of drama, however, closer representation is needed. Silhouettes do not excite our sympathy, even if they behave as we do. If a film is projected under defective lighting conditions, it will (setting aside all other matters of worsened composition, obscuring of detail, and so on) produce a markedly smaller emotional effect, when the human figures become less lifelike.

Synthetic films, even when they aim at the lifelike, fall far short of natural films. This is partly because they are patently flat. The devices of shading, perspective and apparent movement perpendicular to the plane of the screen do not at present give the degree of solidity to which natural films accustom us. This movement of two-dimensional beings in an apparently three-dimensional world, we have termed a dimensional conflict.[1] It is possible that it contributes something of the unreality which the synthetic film is observed to have. But it is clearly not fundamental. In the natural film, a three-dimensional world is represented in two dimensions; in the synthetic film, a two-dimensional world is represented in the same number of dimensions. If, therefore, the normal indications of solidity were present in the synthetic film, a degree of reproductiveness could be obtained as great as, but no greater than, that which the natural film commands. Hence we see that the synthetic film suffers no theoretical limitations whatever in comparison with the natural film. Practically, however, the further complication of the synthetic film would be a very serious matter. The number of drawings which have to be made to render movement smooth will be realized to be very large at a projection-rate of twenty-four frames per second. If each drawing had to be executed with the care necessary to portray the minutiae of shading and movement which go to the making of the natural part of personality, the task of producing even a short synthetic film might exceed all possible undertaking. The mechanical part of the work could be carried out with the aid of skilled assistants; but a very large amount of inspired work would remain,

[1] See p. 34 above.

and inspiration might be crushed by ceaseless repetition.

If these difficulties were only partially overcome, the unexplored scope of the synthetic film would still be very large. There are tales, like that of *Aucassin and Nicolette*, which need a detachment from the world that in literature an old language and the fragrance of romance can give. The force of nature, as the natural film presents it, is too rough for this fragility; which, as it never existed on earth, can only be represented by objects which never so existed. The natural film compels with the near presence of humanity; the synthetic film delights with a distant prospect of it.

15. In thus surveying the scope of the cinema's activities, present and potential, we have encountered, as in every art, a conflict of temperaments. To many the cinema has seemed, not only pre-eminently but solely, an instrument of popular entertainment or social reform. In the first place it commands a greater public than any other art, and has a peculiar vividness and concreteness of appeal; and secondly, it has been born in an age when the necessities of life were so hardly won that art had to be condemned as soon as it became escape. But this is a passing phase from which we are emerging now. It will be necessary in the future not only to keep hold on the actualities of the world, but to recognize the

aspects of life which strain away from and above it. This is a platitude which the most inspired and vital part of the cinema has never apprehended; the documentary film will gain strength by encouraging, as it will fritter its strength by depreciating, the work of its fellows in the field. The extreme realist deals with refractory statistics, the extreme romantic with illusory dreams. The documentary director must learn his facts from the one, and base his appeal on the methods of the other. So compassion, the great social ferment, will disintegrate the evil elements of the old system; while reason, cementer of differing temperaments, will bind the structure of a new. The cinema will not contribute to the mechanism of the new order; but, by building emotion on the basis of thought, it will ease and speed the transition.

Chapter VIII

Conclusion

'Culpable beginnings have found commendable conclusions.'
SIR THOMAS BROWNE: *Christian Morals*

---

1. *The denunciation of the cinema: reply to Mr. Ervine.* 2. *The extravagant praise of the cinema: reply to Eisenstein and Pudovkin.* 3. *The function of criticism in the advancement of the cinema.* 4. *The scope of training studios.*

---

1. We have already suggested that it is premature to assess to-day the place of the cinema among the arts. It is therefore necessary to deprecate extremes of praise and blame; and possible to indicate reasons for adopting some middle course. Mr. St. John Ervine, one of the warmest supporters of the theatre, upholds the merit of his own art largely by decrying the merits of its chief rival. None will deny a proportion of films their travesties of life, their falsity of values and their shallow portrayal of emotion. This was brought out above in the historical section, which did not attempt to disguise the foolishness and worthlessness of a great part of the contemporary cinema. It is no less clear, however, that for fifteen years men of active intelligence

308

have been found ready to devote themselves to the beginnings of an art, accepting a return of aesthetic value and permanence far less than their talents would have received in the service of a maturer medium. This Mr. Ervine ignores. He may in fact know and believe it, concealing his knowledge in order to provoke a reaction from the inert public he chastises. Such would be the attitude of a mere controversialist; but Mr. Ervine, by his great accomplishments in three branches of art, criticism and the writing of novels and plays, has led us to expect a balanced and honest expression of his opinions. If he would give some of his time to acquiring a knowledge of the cinema, his sober judgments would command the utmost weight against the uninformed and irresponsible comments of the film press to-day. The average column of film criticism, even in journals which pride themselves on their appreciation of the arts, could be applied just as well to the stage with no more than a change of heading. Acting alone is appraised, and the director, if he is mentioned at all, is a mere manipulator of the actors. Miss Lejeune, commonly considered our most intelligent film critic, allots seven pages of an essay entitled 'What to Look for in Films' to the credit titles, and only one to the study of the film itself.[1]

[1] See *For Filmgoers Only: The Intelligent Filmgoer's Guide to the Films*.

The star system is as dominant as ever; and those stars who have toured Europe in trousers, or eloped with famous directors, impress themselves on the minds of even the most dignified critics.

Mr. Ervine could discover, if he would, the beginning of a national cinema, though swamped at present by cosmopolitan appeals to sense and sensation; and he might encourage the attention without which it may languish into a mere minority group. It is difficult to know whether art was greatest in the periods when the community made it integral with their lives as citizens and private men; or when it became the prerogative of the few, who developed it to a stage of refinement which the masses could never appreciate. Supporters even of the latter view, however, will not deny that understanding of art is essential to a true scale of values, and that at a time like the present, when the public taste has been cheapened to destruction, art would give the community a new sense of unified life. The cinema has a far greater following than the stage; but the stage is far more often the storehouse of social and artistic values. Mr. Ervine constantly searches out and tries to remedy the causes of the theatre's relative unpopularity; he might also reveal and foster the unmistakable signs of a true national expression in the cinema. Instead he spends himself in denunciation. In an article entitled 'Why I Denounce the Pictures' he wrote: 'If I refer to film fans as celluloid nit-wits, I do not imply that film fans are certifiable lunatics: I do imply that they are people with a low intellectual standard.' Again: 'The moving-picture is mechanically superb and intellectually contemptible.' And: 'Until the moving-picture has naturalized itself in every nation and has become identified with the life of that nation, it cannot be any other than it now is: a sprawling, infantile and mindless thing, offering no hope that it will ever grow a mind.'[1]

2. But the opposite standpoint is equally regrettable. Eisenstein is reported as saying: 'The cinema is the representative art of to-day as painting was of yesterday. Painting is buried. The growth in attendance at art exhibits is a result of publicity and additional newspapers devoting more space to them, and not to a manifestation of a naturally stimulated life.'[2] And Pudovkin: 'Now that I have finished *Deserter* I am sure that sound film is potentially the art of the future. It is not an orchestral creation centring round music, nor yet a theatrical dominated by the factor of the actor, nor even is it akin to opera, it is a synthesis of each and every element—the oral, the visual, the philosophical, it is our opportunity to translate the world in all its lines and shadows into a new art form that has succeeded and will supersede

[1] *The Observer.*
[2] *Experimental Cinema*, no. 4, p. 17.

all the older arts, for it is the supreme medium in which we can express to-day and to-morrow.'[1] To allege that the modern mind is capable of being satisfied by a single art is a criticism rather of the modern mind than of the other arts which men have found necessary to their spiritual growth for many thousand years. It is a piece of remarkable presumption to suppose that because a few intelligent people have turned instinctively to the cinema, and because millions more have looked at films not of their making, the cinema must supersede the other arts. There is no ground whatever for supposing this; there are connoisseurs of music who care nothing for painting, and architects who read only detective stories. Even the more limited claim that the cinema must stand first in a hierarchy of arts cannot possibly be sustained. Putting aside the insuperable difficulty of establishing any such hierarchy on a basis even of informed agreement, the cinema cannot aspire to greatness until it has the backing of a long tradition, and some root in the national life. It is this that the critic, in his endeavour to guide public opinion, must contribute.

3. Criticism must become less catholic, not more. Hitherto any well-meaning attempt to transfer plays to the screen has been praised as a contribution to the cinema. But no more than the Anglican

[1] *Film Technique* (new edn.), pp. 173-174.

Church can admit preachers who deny its central doctrines, and yet keep its integrity, can the cinema remain true to itself while permitting its special powers to be contaminated. Nor must films be degraded to the level of entertainment. Entertainment indeed is an ambiguous term; those who deplore it are accused of a kill-joy puritanism, or an inaccessible and 'highbrow' critical standard; those who commend it certainly refer it to opiates, rather than stimulants. If this be so, it must be tolerated only on sufferance. The tired business man might be thought to have sufficient means of relaxation without the cinema; but if he must be further catered for, it should be made perfectly clear that the films which satisfy him are of an inferior nature. It is not that they transfer him to a world of fantasy, rather than fact; much of the greatest art, and nearly all music, is a resolution of spiritual conflicts rather than a remedy for social ills. It is that his transport to an unreal world is conducted by the simplest appeal to the senses; there is no call upon his imagination, nor upon his thought or deeper emotions.

To insist upon the inferiority of such films, while assessing their worth in this class, and admitting their function in special circumstances; to show that the better films are those which give greater enjoyment to all who bring to them a richer experience of life, and a deeper knowledge of art; to make the

313

cinema as much an expression and an inspiration of national life as the theatre has been in the past, and will be again in the future; these are the tasks of criticism. Its channels must comprise the specialized journals already devoted to it; more important, the daily papers, whose careless ignorance of films contrasts ill with their conscientious and often valuable critiques of novels and plays; above all, the broadcasting system, which has already in other branches of culture so tactfully and ably raised its own standard above the public's, and kept it always a little way ahead.

4. Criticism, however, at best provides an opportunity, rather than forming a cause of artistic greatness. It is the soil and sun, but not the life of the plant. A demand for better films will doubtless promote their supply; but if there is no supply apparently forthcoming from the start, there will be little increased demand. Advance must be very slow; for each party will hesitate, looking for signs of previous activity from the other. There is therefore a need for training studios to be set up, to prepare not for the vast commercialisms of to-day, but for the smaller and more specialized films of the future. Documentary films, in the broadest definition given above, are probably the main prospect of the cinema. They can record, as well as recommend; criticize the existing social structure, or express an attitude

314

which has no educational significance. This is far too broad a field for reliance on the scope of a government department, at any rate in a democratic state; even in Russia the cinema has been unduly restricted by the demands of propaganda. Hence arises the necessity of such studios as we have indicated. They would teach the theory, as well as giving scope for the practice, of making films; for the cinema to-day needs fewer films but harder thinking. It is often said, in the jargon of the trade, that the best 'movie' comes from people who think least, read least and write least about films. This is justified by a confused analogy with other arts, in which the individual can experiment with ease and cheapness until he has secured a combination of words, notes or colours which in some degree satisfies his canons of art and criticism. But the cinema is too expensive a medium to err; if it does so, it must persuade the public to pay for its mistakes. No responsible architect would design a house so that the roof at once began to leak and then explain to his clients that damp was really healthy; he would have made a study of the different stresses which stone, concrete, steel and glass will bear, and of the relative durability of these and other materials. So the film director must give the closest attention in thought to the experiments which economy in part forbids him to execute. The functions of a training studio must therefore comprise theoretical teaching in the structural tools and the modes of appreciation of the cinema, experiment carefully controlled by previous theory, and realization of a standard which the public would by then demand. These studios would be commercial in that they would support themselves financially from the rentals of the films which they exhibited in cinemas; but they would have to shed the falsity and unintelligence which impair the commercial films of to-day.

This programme could not in any case be carried out for many years; it will never be carried out at all unless enlightenment spreads to the public. The critic must prepare this ground; the artist must be ready to take his chance when it comes.

Oxford, 1933-1934

CHART

Reproduction. Representation. Randomness.

Photo-play. Screen-play. Documentary. Imagist film. Abstract.

The Film.

Analysis of structure. → Synthesis of effect.

SOUND. — Speech. Natural sound. Music.

SIGHT. — Content. Alternatives to cut. Literary elements. — Titles.

Alternatives to cut. — Fade. Dissolve. Wipe.

DIFFERENTIATING FACTORS. — Non-optical. Optical.

Non-optical. — Taste. Touch. Smell. Muscular sensations. Mechanism of attention.

OPTICAL. — FILMIC. NATURAL.

NATURAL. — Camera. — Angle. Distance. Position. Close-up.

FILMIC. — STATIC. DYNAMIC.

STATIC. — Delimitation of screen. Composition. Colour. Flatness. Lighting. Stereoscopy.

DYNAMIC. — Pan. Tilt. Track. Film-motion. — Reversal. Fast. Slow. Temporal close-up. Distortion. Lenses. Superimposition. Reduplication. Focus.

IMPLICATIONAL MONTAGE. IDEOLOGICAL MONTAGE.

Sequence.

IDEOLOGICAL MONTAGE. — Sequence. Fixed concept.

IMPLICATIONAL MONTAGE. — Series effect.

Series effect. — Cutting tone. Content tone.

RHYTHMICAL MONTAGE. — $C_1 C_2 C_3 C_4 C_5 ...... C_n$

SECONDARY MONTAGE. — $S_1 S_2 S_3 S_4 ..... S_{n+1}$

PRIMARY MONTAGE. — $S_1 S_2 S_3 S_4 ..... S_{n+1}$

SIMULTANEOUS MONTAGE. — Series.

$S_1 S_2 S_3 S_4 ..... S_{n+1}$ is a succession of shots.

$S_1 S_2 S_3 S_4 ..... S_{n+1}$ is a rhythmical series of sounds, the limits of each sound being defined as temporally coincident with the limits of its accompanying shot.

$C_1 C_2 C_3 C_4 ...... C_n$ is a rhythmical series of cuts dividing the defined succession of shots.

NOTE. The chart should be read downwards from *Analysis of structure* and upwards towards *Synthesis of effect*.

Index

319

Index

Index

Index

Index

Index